THE
PEOPLE

THE
PEOPLE

GROWTH AND SURVIVAL

GERHARD HIRSCHFELD

FOREWORD BY KENNETH E. BOULDING

AldineTransaction
A Division of Transaction Publishers
New Brunswick (U.S.A.) and London (U.K.)

New paperback printing 2008
Copyright © 1973 by the Council for the Study of Mankind, Inc.

This book is printed on acid-free paper that meets the American National Standard for Permanence of Paper for Printed Library Materials.

Library of Congress Catalog Number: 2008018015
ISBN: 978-0-202-36199-4
Printed in the United States of America

Library of Congress Cataloging-in-Publication Data

Hirschfeld, Gerhard, 1897-
  The people : growth and survival / Gerhard Hirschfeld with a foreword by Kenneth E. Boulding.
     p. cm.
  Originally published: Chicago : Aldine Pub. Co., [1973].
  Includes bibliographical references and index.
  ISBN 978-0-202-36199-4
     1. Social history. 2. Cooperation. 3. Leadership. I. Title.

HN8.H47 2008
305.5'1—dc22   2008018015

THE QUESTIONS: FIRST CYCLE

The two most important questions, of course, are "Will
mankind survive?" and "How can we ensure that it will —
that *we* will?" This book is an attempt to open a far-reaching
discussion of these questions — among many people — by
providing a background for that discussion and by posing
questions we hope will contribute to that discussion. Toward
this goal, you will find enclosed in this book an envelope
addressed to the Council for the Study of Mankind, who have
sponsored the book's publication. (If the envelope has been
removed by another reader, we would appreciate a letter with
(1) your comments on the book and/or any responses to the
questions posed in Kenneth Boulding's Foreword, (2) your
name and address if you would like a free subscription to the
Council's *Bulletin*, where all reactions to this book will be
reported. Address: Council for the Study of Mankind, Box
6926, Chicago, Illinois 60680.)

We here at the Council for the Study of Mankind, then,
invite all readers of this book to join a discussion which for
the past quarter century has engaged only a few hundred
scholars around the world. We ask that in the enclosed

envelope, or in a letter, you send us your own contribution to the discussion. Your responses will be reported in the Council's *Bulletin* (which you may obtain free of charge), and they will be incorporated in the next printing — the Second Cycle — of *The People: Growth and Survival.*

This book has three parts. The main part is Gerhard Hirschfeld's contribution to the question of how it is that we the people have historically and to the present time always received less than our fair share of the earth's goods and privileges. This is most of the book, and the floor is open — without limitation — for discussion of any of the theses presented in it. Then there is an appended program of action, beginning on page 177, which suggests how we the people might reverse the historic trend, redress the balance, and give ourselves — all of humankind — our due. A third part of the book is the Foreword by Kenneth Boulding, which poses questions raised in *his* mind by the central problems discussed in the main part of the book. Every reader is invited to respond to these same questions or to comment independently.

In human affairs, of course, the name of the game is not the reaching of single, "correct" answers to difficult questions, but rather the process of first posing the difficult questions and then finding and discussing alternative answers to them.

The discussion of problems concerning all of humankind cannot be very fruitful if it takes place among only a small group. To the contrary, the discussion beginning with this book must spread as quickly as possible through peoples of very different languages and perspectives — old and young, poor and rich — of all the earth's varied cultures. It is a task without end — and any who become impatient with such a prospect are reminded of Oliver Wendell Holmes' response when asked how it felt to have reached the age of ninety: that he preferred it to the alternative.

Behind us are at least two million years of the evolution of a genus some of whose members "make changes" that seem good enough to others to persuade them to follow. Here we are now, caught up in change so fast and wide- spread that it appears to many that most of our future is behind us. The time is past when disastrous experiments were confined to small groups which could be sacrificed for the whole. Now the species, still confined to "spaceship earth," may be wholly consumed as a result of the actions of only a few of its members. This was foreseen most clearly by the international group of scientists who first released atomic energy in Chicago 30 years ago; and it was there that the Council for the Study of Mankind was founded. (In those innocent days it was assumed by males that the English word "man" included both sexes and that "mankind" was *Homo sapiens,* the human species.) The motto of the Council became and remains:

> Today, mankind for the first time is emerging as a communicating and potentially cooperating society. This process creates great opportunity as well as great danger. To help exploit the one and avert the other, the Council proposes to study human society as a whole and to stimulate re-thinking of concepts and values in terms of the future of that society.
>
> For 25 years we have been sympathetic intellectuals content to talk to one another, but clearly our group and its limited efforts are unequal to a task that demands the whole-hearted efforts and actions of all mankind. The time has come to bring into the conversation all of the people, and this book is a beginning.

Sol Tax, Chairman
Council for the Study of Mankind

THE COUNCIL FOR THE STUDY OF MANKIND, INC.

x

xi

FOREWORD

Gerhard Hirschfeld is the best example I know of a
principle that I have been calling "Nag's law" — that is, all
good things come by nagging. It is not the flash of brilliance,
or even the outburst of creative expression that really
changes the world. It is the nagger who really changes things
— the man who will not take no for an answer, who keeps at
it day in and day out, whose strength is as the strength of ten
because his heart is pure, who is importunate like the widow
in the parable, who has a vision that cannot be denied and
who therefore will not be denied. The great principle of the
unity of mankind, to which many of us give lip service, or
which we glimpse fitfully and occasionally, Hirschfeld takes
as his pole star, follows it all his waking hours, and I wouldn't
be surprised if he dreams about it at night. He pesters people
until in sheer desperation they do what he asks them to do
because he is irresistible. His purity and his singlemindedness
drive us all forward, and when we have done what he wants
us to do, we perceive that it was right. He has acted upon his
vision while we have sat at ease in Zion, and the world will
never be quite the same again.

Few people will agree with all of this book, but only the

most insensitive will fail to be moved by it. Like every prophetic statement and every vision of the future that amounts to anything, it begins with a vision of the past. It is a vision of a long travail of mankind. (Careful, Gerhard, half the race is womankind; we had better make it humankind!) Humankind, then, is divided into three parts. There is first the "people," those who are everlastingly pushed around, who create opportunity by the sheer breeding of more people and by producing a surplus. Then there are the "leaders," those who seize the opportunity provided by the surplus and with it make nations, fight wars, produce art and religion. The third are the "middle class," those who develop and refine what leaders create and originate, and who expand with development at the expense of the other two. What the leaders really exploit is opportunity, though in the process the people get exploited too. Opportunity is created by conflict, even by war, by invention, by development.

Now the message is — there is another opportunity. Development has proceeded to the point where one world is not only possible, but necessary. It is by the seizing of this last great opportunity that the liberation of the people from age-long oppression and servitude becomes possible. The people, however, almost by definition, cannot take advantage of opportunity. We must therefore convert the leaders and mobilize the seizers of opportunity to seize this greatest opportunity of all.

There is something of Goldsmith's village parson about Gerhard Hirschfeld. Those who come to scoff remain, if not to pray, at least to work and think. He says, in effect, to the intellectual and academic community — these are the real problems of the world, why aren't you working on them? There is no answer to this question, except to go to work on them.

A book of this kind should raise more questions than it answers, and this one does. Each reader should raise questions of his own. The ones that follow are mine. They are real questions, that is, questions to which the questioner does not know the answer rather than rhetorical questions, questions to which the questioner thinks he knows the answer and expects the reader to supply the right one.

Question 1. Have we crossed, or are we about to cross some fundamental watershed in the history of the human race which represents a change in the basic parameters of the world social system so that the previous patterns, such as those described in the first ten chapters of this book, do not necessarily apply?

Question 2. Even if we are passing through a "systems break," as suggested in the first question, how much carryover is there from the processes of the past, and are there any necessary patterns, whether evolutionary, dialectical, or other, in the processes of social dynamics which carry us onward through time in society?

Question 3. Is it the integration of the "noosphere" (the sphere of knowledge all around the world) that is forcing us into mankind-consciousness with the expansion of travel, communication, and so on (it probably is), and if so, can we understand better the evolutionary or dialectical processes by which the "noosphere" expands and changes, and can we understand how the cognitive content of human nervous sytems is transformed?

Question 4. How do we define the concept of mankind interest? Is there anything indeed which is good or bad for mankind as a whole?

Question 5. If we can define a mankind interest, how far can we reconcile this with personal, group, class, race, national, religious, and other sectional interests?

Question 6. Do we want a homogeneous world culture, and what value do we place on variety in human culture? If we value variety, what steps can be taken to preserve it within the framework of a mankind interest? What case is there for a humane and legitimated system of "apartheid" to preserve the diversity and the variety of human cultures? How far can we fractionate the individual person into different roles and diverse cultures?

Question 7. Can we identify, better than we do now, the distributional aspects of human decisions, especially powerful decisions? Any decision presumably divides mankind into three groups — those who are favorably affected, those who are unfavorably affected, and those who are unaffected. Can we identify these groups better than we do now? If we can, would this favor or injure the development of a mankind interest?

Question 8. What kind of implicit social contract is involved in the concept of a mankind interest? Can this be spelled out and can it be embodied in an explicit social contract in the form of a world constitution?

The U.S. Constitution, which will certainly go down in history as one of the more successful social contracts, was the outcome of a hundred years of hard political thinking and discussion. If we are to develop a viable constitution for the human race, we need another such period of intense political thought, communication, and interaction among all the various political species that inhabit the "noosphere." This book is a contribution to this interaction and is one more push toward the "systems break" we are seeking.

Kenneth E. Boulding

PREFACE

One problem has been of deep concern to me for a long time: why it has never been possible for all the people of any land in any age and under any conditions to attain freedom, security, and self-determination in a measure commensurate with human dignity. The purpose of this book is not to find a solution to this question but to investigate the nature of the problem.

One segment of the population in particular has been denied the attributes of human dignity. This group, which I call "the people," forms the great majority in any economically motivated, politically organized collective, such as a community, city, state, or nation. These people occupy the lower strata of society in terms of income and education, and for a variety of reasons, they have been more subject than others to the exploitation of bosses, employers, financiers, presidents, kings, barons, feudal lords, tribal chiefs, religious, political, academic, cultural, and other leaders.

The term "exploitation" refers to a situation in which advantage is taken (the dictionary calls it "selfish or unfair utilization") of a person without providing adequate compensation or an alternate choice in terms of social and cultural standards. Exploitation occurs when the peasant loses his land because he cannot pay the taxes assessed by his employers; when the faithful must accept the doctrine of the church or face excommunication; when the member of a minority group is refused employment; when a worker is forced to accept substandard wages because the alternative is no wages at all; when the union member is told to strike or lose his membership; when the citizen is ordered to go to war or go to jail.

In this context, three generalizations can be made about "the people." First, they make up the bulk of any large economically motivated, politically organized collective; second, they are dependent upon others for a living, and have little choice as to the terms and conditions of their employment; and third, largely because of economic pressures, they have neither time nor taste for other serious endeavors, especially in the political field.

Since this essay is a rather brief historical survey, with more emphasis upon depth than breadth, one must expect the definitions, whatever they are, to be broad and indefinite. The reader is asked, therefore, to make concessions. Whenever one deals with the broad sweep of history, one must forego the great mass of detail.

In fact, it may not be possible or even necessary to define "the people" as one defines classes or categories. Can we define "life" or the "universe" or "electricity" or the "individual person" or "nature" in any precise way? These are not really things or subjects. They are phenomena.

The same is true of "the people." The dependent, often mis-informed, half- or un-educated, insecure, exploited masses are a phenomenon, a constantly shifting, changing element which refuses to be tied to a precise definition or squeezed into a particular mold. Could one point to any period in history or to any country at any time and say: "These are the people!"? Any definition will cover some but not all of them, perhaps not even a substantial majority. The group is so complex, irregular, and unstable as it moves through the various stages of history with its fluctuations in cultural, social, institutional, economic, and political forms and values that it seems an impossible task to try to define it.

And yet, there appears to be a clear and definite set of characteristics (apart from those mentioned above) that makes the people stand out as a solid and cohesive factor through the ages. There is a particular behavior pattern that responds not so much to advertising slogans and campaign promises as to basic needs and realities—a response that never varies, as of a hungry person to a paying job, of a lonely male to an attractive female, of a searching follower to an inspiring leader. The person who responds to commercials and ready promises may change his or her mind—from a Cadillac to a Ford, from vitamins to dumbbells, from the *Yale Review* to the *New·Yorker*, from sex to hi-fi, from outdoor movies to the public library. In contrast, on the basic issues the people in general have little or no choice. They *must* take a job— they have to eat. They *must* go on strike—the union says so. They *must* believe in God—it is the right thing to do. They *must* go to war—the government insists.

In view of these seemingly inflexible societal relationships, the question arises whether there are laws of nature involved that control the behavior of the people and about which man can do little or nothing. If the people's basic response never varies, regardless of the forces to which they are exposed, does this imply that anything that is done in the traditional concepts and old-fashioned ways to change the people and their lot, is doomed to failure? If such laws exist, do they account for the subordinate role the people have played in history? By what devices, then, could a basic improvement of their place in society be attained? What might be the magic formula, if any, that would erase major obstacles and give new hope that dignity for all men might soon become a reality?

An inquiry into the history of the people is presented in the pages that follow. If lack of knowledge of and lack of interest in the affairs of the collective is not and never has been characteristic of the people everywhere, what accounts for their exploitation and suppression? On the other hand, if the people are not meant by the laws of nature to be economically independent or politically free, is freedom for the people an idle hope, and is democracy or communism or any other ism an illusion? A prime purpose of this book is to seek to explain why in all history the people have never attained lasting freedom, security, and self-determination—briefly, dignity.

The future of political institutions is related to these larger questions. If the people are compelled to go to war, and if democracy plays a decisive part in it, then something better than the kind of democracy we know is obviously needed. If communism is responsible for withholding from the people any semblance of freedom and self-determination, the obvious need is for something better than the kind of communism we know today. The need might then be to develop the ideas underlying democracy and communism upon a higher level where their admittedly similar basic aims—to improve the status of the people—would meet on common ground, thus making possible a common approach.

Once we know the reasons for the past failures of the people to attain freedom and self-determination, we should be closer to a possible solution to the existing problems. Most assuredly, we do not lack individuals fervently devoted to the betterment of the people. Social thinkers have held out the hope that, with the continued advance of civilization, their lot could and would be improved. Yet, the great majority of the people today in Asia, Africa, Latin America, and other continents, seem no nearer to economic security or political freedom than were the people in the past.

Faced with these problems, all of which are marked by great variety, great complexity, and great urgency, I feel that we should not be too impatient for a solution. First, we must do some basic thinking. To help in this prior task is the purpose of this book.

ACKNOWLEDGMENTS

Appreciation for counsel and guidance is due to many. Special thanks are due to those with whom I have discussed through the years the problems dealt with in this book. They share the author's concern for the future of Mankind, but not necessarily either his general views or particular interpretations:

Theodore Brameld
John I. Goodlad
Bert F. Hoselitz
Richard P. McKeon
Aaron Scheinfeld
Sol Tax
Robert Ulich
W. Warren Wagar
Quincy Wright

To my wife, whose faith, collaboration, and understanding lightened the heavy load, I am deeply grateful.

CONTENTS

CHAPTER
ONE

THE
PEOPLE
AS
CREATORS
OF
OPPORTUNITY

Without the people, basic opportunity for the development of civilization would not exist. By the "basic opportunity" I mean the forces that sweep up the old, thus making room for the new. This opportunity causes the collapse of economic systems, political orders, and social eras, and leads to the emergence of new forms of government, new patterns of achievement, new means of creating wealth, new ways of living, and new standards of conformity. It means major upheavals rather than surface manifestations. Therefore, the importance of opportunity is as much in its period of inception and incubation as in its eventual realization. Cause and effect may be centuries apart and not readily evident, but seen in their proper perspective it is possible to trace the forces that make for new opportunity and to see them in a meaningful pattern.

The people create new opportunity chiefly in two ways: through congregating in places that seem advantageous, thereby developing community life; and through a high birth rate, favored by the thriving cities and in turn stimulating further growth. Towns rise because the people multiply, and the people multiply because the cities expand. Generally, towns and cities have neither risen nor expanded in the absence of a growing population. Medieval Europe is a case in point.

In the valleys of inner Europe, the medieval peasants lived an isolated existence. Not overly important to Europe's economic progress, they worked in the shadow of the castle under the baron's protection. Their economic effort was small, its dynamic quality low, its scope narrow. The promise of new wealth scarcely existed. Nor did the people seek to congregate for common gain. Few cities grew.

A different situation existed along the coastline. Thousands of people crossed the desert, the mountains, and the sea to reach that blessed bit of land where commerce flourished in spectacular fashion. Opportunity was ripe for enterprise. Dynamic growth engulfed the sea-bordering states of England, Holland, Spain, Portugal, and Italy. Cities amassed great wealth. The economic effort was intense, its dynamic quality high, its scope "global." New towns grew, and with them new commerce, new economic interests, new political demands, new artistic forms, new cultural patterns. Such growth and dynamic activity would not have been likely without the people who filled the towns and cities, buying and selling, producing and consuming, saving and exchanging, going to church and serving their masters.

PREDISPOSING CAUSES OF NEW OPPORTUNITY

A good long-range view of predisposing causes can be seen in European history since the seventeenth century. The predisposing causes of the English Revolution may have preceded its actual outbreak by nearly two hundred years. The Wars of the Roses ended in 1461 with the victory of Towton Field and with Edward IV on the throne of England. The victory put an end to the liberty of Parliament and established the rule of the Crown.

Although other factors played a part, the underlying cause of that conflict was the rise of the town. The Wars of the Roses were followed by a period marked by the expansion of manufacturing and the widening of markets. Led by the manufacture of textiles, industry began to grow. The new industrialists found it easier to employ people and to operate plants outside of the established towns where the guilds insisted upon strict regulation and control of manufacturing activities. As a result, many new towns and villages sprang up.[1]

Even more important were the merchants who ventured upon the seas. As the English merchants, strongly supported by the Crown, steadily developed their markets and improved their organization, the powerful Italian and Venetian merchants and especially the Hanseatic League began to give ground. By the close of Edward IV's reign in 1483, it is estimated that native merchants controlled 88 per cent of the wool trade, 59 per cent of the export in cloth, 65 per cent of the merchandise paying tunnage and poundage, and over 75 per cent of wine imports.[2]

Based upon shipping and trading activities in the Cinque Ports on the Channel as well as in London, Bristol, and other towns, the new wealth of seaborne commerce asserted itself against the entrenched wealth of the Church. Pursuing new economic interests, mostly abroad, the owners of the new wealth increasingly claimed economic and political rights, mostly at home. The refusal to give in to these claims eventually led to the defeat of the Crown and the death of Charles I in 1649.[3]

New opportunity is usually marked by the following chain of events: (1) the people congregate in favorably situated places around which towns and cities develop; (2) commerce and industry flourish, leading to increased population and new wealth; (3) the owners of new wealth make demands upon the owners of old wealth for more rights and greater privileges; (4) eventually, the new powers take control of the affairs of state.

POPULATION INCREASE

The increase of the population in England and on the continent was marked during the sixteenth and seventeenth centuries. At the beginning of the sixteenth century, Europe counted six or seven cities with more than 100,000 inhabitants. At the end of the century, there were thirteen or fourteen such cities.[4]

However, the population increase attained its full momentum only in the eighteenth and nineteenth centuries, as shown in table 1.

TABLE 1
Population Increase of European Countries, 1480 to 1880

	1480	1680	1780	1880
England and Wales	3,700,000	5,532,000	9,561,000	35,002,000
France	12,600,000	18,800,000	25,100,000	37,400,000
Prussia	800,000	1,400,000	5,460,000	45,260,000*
Austria	9,500,000	14,000,000	20,200,000	37,830,000
Russia	2,100,000	12,600,000	26,800,000	84,440,000
Italy	9,200,000	11,500,000	12,800,000	28,910,000

*After unification

During the nineteenth century, vast commercial expansion and New World conquests combined with progress in medicine, sanitation, and hygiene to cause tremendous population growth. This change is reflected in the increase in the number of European cities having 100,000 or more inhabitants. In 1850, there were 42 such cities; in 1870, 70; in 1895, 120.[5]

To say that throughout history the people have provided the basic opportunity for growth is stating the obvious. Family and community, tribe and nation, race and religion, culture and institution, would hardly have had the opportunity to exist, let alone to grow, if there had not been the people. Why, then, state the obvious? I am concerned here not with the basic importance of the presence of the people but with certain implications and consequences arising from that fact. Thinkers in past as in modern times have rarely talked about the people as the providers of basic opportunity for growth, but almost always about the implications and possible consequences arising from that opportunity, or their absence.

H. G. Wells, in discussing the chief elements in the accumulation of human beings that made up the later Babylonian and Egyptian civilizations, says:

> At the base of the social pyramid was the large and most necessary class in the community, *the tillers of the soil.* . . . and so the cultivator class is generally a poorly educated, close-toiling class, superstitious by reason of ignorance and the uncertainty of the seasons, ill-informed and easily put upon. It is capable at times of great passive resistance, but it has no purpose in its round but crops and crops, to keep out of debt and hoard against bad times. So it has remained to our own days over the greater part of Europe and Asia.[6]

5

Leslie A. White, in discussing the early development of agricultural technology, says:

> As the food supply was enlarged, the population increased. Small tribes grew into large tribes and these into nations and empires; villages grew into towns and towns into cities. . . . The mere increase in population had important consequences in another direction also. Tribes and clans were organized upon a basis of kinship ties; social relations were largely exercised in this form . . . . But when, under the impetus of a developing agricultural technology and an increasing food supply, clan and tribal units grew to huge size, they tended to fall apart of their own weight . . . . A new type of social organization was therefore required if chaos was to be averted. This new organization was found in the State.[7]

Arnold J. Toynbee says:

> What then is the right way of describing the relation between human societies and individuals? The truth seems to be that a

human society is, in itself, a system of relationships between human beings who are not only individuals but are also social animals in the sense that they could not exist at all without being in this relationship to one another. A society, we may say, is a product of the relations between individuals, and these relations of theirs arise from the coincidence of their individual fields of action. This coincidence combines the individual fields into a common ground, and this common ground is what we call a society. . . . If this definition is accepted, an important though obvious corollary emerges from it. Society is a "field of action" but the *source* of all action is in the individuals composing it.[8]

Pierre Teilhard de Chardin says:

After rising slowly until the seventeenth century, when it reached about 400 millions, the earth's population began to shoot up in an alarming fashion. It was 800 millions by the end of the eighteenth century, 1,600 millions by 1900, and over 2,000 millions by 1940. At the present rate of increase, regardless of war and famine, we must expect a further 500 millions in the next 25 years. This demographic explosion, so closely connected with the development of a relatively unified and industrialized Earth, clearly gives rise to entirely new necessities and problems, both quantative and qualitative.[9]

M. M. Kovalevsky, the Russian sociologist (1851-1916), saw in the growth and density of population the most constant impulse to social and economic development. Long before old classes are dethroned and rulers forced to abdicate, the people, through multiplication, concentration, migration, as well as through the development of new habits, desires, aspirations, political demands, and other processes, have influenced the course of social conditions, economic developments, and political changes:

I have attempted to determine the influence of the density of population on the changes in the organization of production and exchange and on the structure of property. This factor has been responsible for the transition from a stage of hunters and fishermen to one of agriculture, and from a primitive system of agriculture to a more intensive one, with corresponding changes in the system of land ownership and land possession. . . . The substitution of a manufacturing system of production in industry for a domestic one is due to the same factor. . . . Thus, the simple fact of the growth of population called forth a division of labor, a social differentiation into castes, orders and classes, and the evolution of the technique of production, as well as that of the economic regime.[10]

These are some of the observations about and implications of the link between population increase and the opportunity for growth. Other questions, perhaps less frequently asked, are no less important:

(1) If people have proved so important in providing the basic opportunity for growth, in which ways and to what extent have they been rewarded in different ages, in different countries, under different conditions? If they have been rewarded, why is the majority of the people living today in conditions of poverty, disease, exploitation, and suppression? If they have not been rewarded, should they be?

(2) Is the role of the people in the past history of Europe the same in the more recent history of the United States, as well as in the contemporary history of the developing countries in Asia, Africa, and Latin America?

(3) Is the record of the impact of population growth in the past any indication of the nature, extent, and intensity of its anticipated impact in the future? Or is modern technological advance likely to change the pattern of the future? Or, to go one step further, is perhaps a law of nature involved which, while allowing a great variety of diverse forms, will dictate a future pattern unchanged in basic principles from that of the past?

ECONOMIC IMPACT OF POPULATION GROWTH

Population increase and the accompanying growth of towns and cities had important consequences for economic, political, and social development in Europe. In England, the expansion of commerce led to the extensive building and launching of ships which in turn caused greater demand for domestic coal. Pits were dug deeper but water broke into the stopes; horsepower was too expensive for pumping; the steam-driven pump made its appearance; the output of the mines rose. Steam power was applied to other uses. Business men in England began to manufacture power-driven machinery at about the time of the American Revolution. The initial period of power-driven machinery lasted from 1765 to 1785. Savery's steam engine, Cort's puddling furnace and rolling mill, Watt's shaft-rotating engine, the spinning jenny and the power loom, the Brunswick type of sea-going ship—these were some of the tools forged for the exploitation of economic opportunity.[11, 12]

It may be argued that these and similar developments were the result of a "total" situation, that many factors other than the people should be cited. This is true, yet, as long as we speak of predisposing causes, we must list population growth among the first. Inventions like those just mentioned were the product of genius, but genius was given its opportunity through the forces released by population growth. The evolution of a new continent and the shrinking of an ocean required the invention of the telegraph. More people making more money and seeing more of each other wanted more and better clothes; thus the invention of the sewing machine. Other demands and needs produced the reaper, centrifugal pump, automobile, vacuum cleaner, and radio in the world of yesterday. Tomorrow, they may bring forth the wheel-less train, the wall-less house, air-conditioned clothing, and other products barely envisioned today.

CULTURAL IMPACT

So broad and deep was the economic impact of these changes that it assumed a pattern throughout the Western society. The fact that identical or similar discoveries were often made by several persons independently testifies to the breadth and depth of this pattern.[13] Morse is credited with the invention of the telegraph in 1837, but Henry had turned out a workable machine six years earlier, and Cooke-Wheatstone and Steinheil are said to have made the same discovery in 1837. The sewing machine was invented by Thimmonier in 1830, six years before by Hunt, and fourteen years later by Howe. The centrifugal pump owed its existence to the work of Appold, Gwynne, and Bessemer, all of whom produced their invention in the same year, 1850.[14]

The connection between population concentration and cultural advance by way of discovery and invention is so basic a principle in the development of human society that its operation can be shown in periods thousands of years apart. Population density in ancient China required an elaborately planned technology basically like modern Western technology. China's military road system was so well designed that it was introduced in Europe a little over a century ago.[15]
The people of ancient China knew how to print, to weave cloth, to use wood and stone for building; they had instruments with which to measure. They, or the Mongols, invented explosives. They used a calendar showing the years, months, and days.

The history of the nineteenth century is largely the result of population fertility. Perhaps one cannot remove Napoleon and still retain the political atmosphere needed to explain nineteenth-century European history; another great leader might have produced a different version. But it seems quite certain that with or without Napoleon (or any other spectacular leader), Europe's population would have multiplied, its cities grown, commerce thrived, industry expanded, competition flourished, and labor suffered.

But one can hardly remove such a figure as Karl Marx without replacing him with someone akin in mind and vision. He was the product of conditions caused by fertility, urban concentration, and industrialization, by wealth and luxury, slums and poverty. One can not cross off names like Liebig, Krupp, Pasteur, Rathenau, Rhodes, Rothschild, Volta, because the challenge of new opportunity would not have been met without these or like men. The profound changes engendered by fertility and subsequent population problems cried for great chemists, manufacturers, colonizers, financiers, physicists, statesmen, and revolutionaries. The vision, ambition, determination, struggle, ability, and sacrifice of these and other men and women—applied in the name of new opportunity, new achievement, new wealth, new benefits and, yes, new suffering—are vital factors in the history of nineteenth-century Europe.

POLITICAL IMPACT

While population increase was not confined to England, its impact upon the economic development was, at least for a time. England held tightly to her advantage in the development of new machinery. A ban was placed upon the export of all new machines and was not rescinded until 1825—about 60 years after the introduction of power-driven machinery. Although some of the new wonders appeared in France and the Lowlands, it was not until the ban was lifted that the new machines were found in substantial numbers in northern France and western Germany, and in Vienna, Warsaw, or Budapest. These cities and countries were 40 years behind England, and it took them nearly a century to make up lost time.[16]

The social conditions created by the increase in population and subsequent developments in the nineteenth century not only accentuated the need for new products and new markets but also led to the rise of new classes—foremost among them the working classes. In the process, the power of ruling classes and, eventually, of governments was weakened, sometimes destroyed.

In England, these conditions contributed to the deterioration of the upper class during the latter part of the eighteenth and the early part of the nineteenth century.[17] New leaders able to anticipate the course of economic development and capable of guiding the creation of new wealth came to the fore. English foreign policy, which had failed to heed the signs of economic change in the years preceding the American Revolution, underwent a process of revision and rejuvenation.

On the continent, the emergence of the machine age caused violent repercussions. In 1830, the Belgian people rose to proclaim their independence. In Hanover, Saxony, and other German states, uprisings resulted in greater civil and political liberties. In Italy, the rebels were at first defeated by Austrian troops. But soon there was another and greater revolution, not only in Italy but throughout Europe and across the sea in the countries of Latin America.[18]

GENERAL APPLICATION

Did the people play a similar role in the rest of the world? Bearing in mind differences in time, environment, and rate of development, I would answer in the affirmative. Others would deny it. They would point out that in modern times population growth has not always created new opportunity. The population in Russia was 26,800,000 in 1780, and 84,440,000 a century later. In the colonies and dependencies of the developed nations, the population increased by over 100,000,000 between 1860 and 1920. Specifically, in 40 years of British rule (1882 to 1922), the population of Egypt doubled. In about 50 years of French rule, the population of Algeria doubled. Under the American flag, the Philippine Islands increased their population by about 5,000,000 in 25 years. The population of India grew by 50,000,000 in 40 years; that of the Federated Malay States doubled in 20 years; that of Java totaled about 46,000,000 in 1945, over ten times that of 1800.[19]

In none of these countries has the growth in population been accompanied by the creation of opportunity or a dynamic development of economic resources. Their people have lived in poverty and neglect for years or even decades during the period of population growth. While the population picture by itself may have been favorable to the development of dynamic opportunity, other conditions were not. Taken by itself, population growth can cancel out economic opportunity by making labor so cheap that the use of machinery becomes unprofitable and therefore unattractive. A virtual slave system made the machine as unwelcome in nineteenth-century Russia as in the South before the American Civil War.

The ancient Greeks and Romans were technically ready for some of the eighteenth-century inventions but their social conditions were not. They invented a kind of steam engine but limited its use to religious rituals. The Romans knew the possibilities of explosives, the elevator system, and other modern devices, but did not put them to wide economic use. The abundance of slave labor made conditions unfavorable for the application of machinery.[20] Inventive genius turned to the decorative side of life, to the arts—in Greece as well as in Rome.

But did not a similar situation prevail in eighteenth-and nineteenth-century Europe? Was there not a considerable time lag between population growth and dynamic economic development in the period from 1780 to 1880? The initial period of power-driven machinery, it was stated before, lasted from 1765 to 1785, yet its economic effect did not make itself felt on the continent for another century. The parallel in the time lag between population growth and the dynamic economic development in the nineteenth and twentieth century appears self-evident.

12

Dynamic forces do not seem to manifest themselves simultaneously with population growth; rather, they are generated gradually over an extended period of time. It takes time for an expanding population to build towns and cities, to evolve law and government, to work out a system of agriculture, to produce the sinews of transportation, commerce, and industry, to develop an awareness of the country's growing importance among nations, as well as the concepts and policies commensurate with that importance. Above all, it takes time to develop effective leadership.

Certainly, rapid population increase in the newly developing countries was not accompanied by dynamic economic growth within the same period. Group life in Egypt, Algeria, the Philippine Islands, India, Java, and other countries did not become dynamic as soon as population began to grow. However, everyone of these countries is beginning to show the impact of population growth in varying measure. The movement that led to the independence of the Philippine

Islands; the creation of the Indian and Indonesian republics; the seething unrest throughout Latin America; the emergence of a score of new nations in Africa; the concentration of power in several Arab states (practically all since the end of the Second World War) would not have been likely without the social, economic, and political evolution made possible by the growth of population during and after the second half of the nineteenth century.

OTHER VIEWS

In observing the emergence of a vigorous society and the factors leading to it, noted sociologists (Ludwig Gumplowicz, Gustav Ratzenhofer, Ludwig Stein, and others) attach major importance to conditions of social contact. Their careful studies of social evolution lead them to the general conclusion that the clash of cultures is probably the major factor in breaking down old forms of life, stimulating the imagination, generating new vistas and hopes, and imparting a general vigor which finds expression in population growth as well as in advances in other areas. Rather than regarding new opportunities as a consequence of population growth, many sociologists point out that the opposite is true, namely, that new opportunity leads to population growth.

There is no question that once new opportunity is created it has a powerful impact upon population growth, be it through a higher birth rate, a lower death rate, migration, or all three factors. However, the original technological advance, or any other advance that calls forth the new opportunity, is made possible by the population factor.

Population growth may occur without technical or cultural advance, but technical or cultural advance is unlikely without population growth. During the greater part of human history, technical and cultural advances have been few and far between. Yet, population increased slowly and steadily through the centuries. In our century, many segments of mankind (tribes in different parts of Asia, Africa, Latin America,

13

Australia, and Oceania) increased their numbers steadily even though there was little technical and cultural advance. Although the progress of civilization and technology will substantially accelerate the rate of population growth in these areas, in the meantime, the slow build-up of population has formed the necessary foundation for subsequent technical and cultural development.

This process applies equally to advanced and to newly developing countries. People would hardly congregate in one place, build houses, start new enterprises, develop commerce and industry unless they saw an opportunity for profit and advancement. People built communities because they were assured of the baron's protection, because a crossroad attracted commerce, because gold nuggets were found in the river, because the land was fertile, because the government so decreed, or because the new land offered freedom from persecution. These communities may have provided new opportunities for people as individuals, but they did not always lead to dynamic enterprise for the group.

A different kind of opportunity arose after the towns and cities had been built by large numbers of people. It did not stop with the functional life of a village at the foot of a castle or a town at the confluence of two rivers but created powerful interests and generated strong aspirations among the people as well as their leaders. In short, it generated the dynamic movement that caused major changes in societal living.

States and nations have never grown large in population but stayed forever small in importance and commercial enterprise. This is not to say that small towns or communities cannot engage in dynamic enterprise; large cities and groups have often grown out of dynamic enterprise on a small scale. Nevertheless, two conclusions about dynamic growth can be drawn:

(1) Dynamic societal development requires an active and growing population. Christianity, the French Revolution, the labor movement, and Zionism, would hardly have succeeded upon an inactive and indifferent population.

(2) A densely populated area will eventually generate those forces which, by their dynamic character, tend to bring about the conditions of social conflict as a major factor in the emergence of a vigorous society.

Therefore, it would seem that, although neither population growth nor new opportunity created by technical or cultural advance can produce effective results without the other, population growth must be rated as a basic condition of and therefore a primary factor in the dynamic development of society.

IMPORTANCE OF POPULATION DECLINE

As population growth creates opportunity for the development of society, a decline in population tends to reverse the process, forecasting a long-range decline of the nation. Aside from war and other catastrophes, the process of decline is marked by migration, increase in the aged population, and a decline in the birth rate.

15

MIGRATION

The oppressive rule of the nobles, and the resulting poverty of peasants drove many Greek families to seek new homes beyond the Aegean world between 700 and 600 BC. What Greece lost, the Mediterranean basin was to gain. Greek farmers settled around the Black Sea, along the coast of Asia Minor, in southern Italy, in southern France, and along the eastern coast of Spain. This migration was one predisposing cause of a revolution involving a large part of the world (as the Greeks knew it), and it laid a foundation upon which the Roman Empire was eventually built. The exodus of Greek farmers removed the pillars that were the strength of ancient Greece.[21]

Seventeenth-century England owed many of her industrial

arts, and not a little of the lifeblood of her empire, to the skill of the Huguenots and Flemish immigrants.[22] Scotland and Ireland lost many of their people through migration during the latter half of the nineteenth century. Large numbers of natives were driven from the land by the lords. "Under the laws of eviction over 200,000 homes were destroyed in Ireland during the lifetime of Queen Victoria, or were rendered tenantless for the recovery of civil debts or to clear the inmates off the land to make room for cattle."

The Scots did not fare any better. The lords succeeded in preserving Scotland in the grouse-shooting tradition, but lost many a good man to America. Many Irish joined the exodus. Between 1851 and 1910, more than four million Irish emigrated. During roughly the same period, more than ten million people sailed from England for new shores and new opportunities.[23]

INCREASE OF THE AGED POPULATION

16   Since the end of the Second World War, the birth rate throughout the world has risen sharply. So has the proportion of the aged in the population. In the United States, notwithstanding the substantial rate of population growth since 1945, the trend of an over-all declining rate may be seen in the growing proportion of the aged population:

> .... Today[1955], there are more older people numerically, and in proportion to the population, than ever before. The number of persons 65 years and over in the USA has increased from 1,000,000 in 1870 to about 13,000,000 today. In 1900, the proportion of men and women 65 years of age in our total population was 1 in 25. Today it is about 1 in 12 and is steadily increasing. .... The aged population will continue to grow rapidly in the years ahead. The Bureau of the Census expects that the number of persons aged 65 and over will increase from 13,400,000 in 1953 to 20,700,000 in 1975, and to more than 26,000,000 before the end of the century.[24]

DECLINE IN YOUNGER POPULATION

The increase in the number of aged persons is accompanied by a corresponding decline in the number of young persons in the United States. In 1852, more than 52 per cent of the population were under twenty years of age. In 1930, the percentage had dropped to 40; in 1950, to 32. [25] Economist J. J. Spengler of Duke University says:

> Among developed countries the United States is relatively young. Some 30 percent of the poulation is less than 15 years old—not as high a proportion as the 37 percent world average, but greater than that of the U. S. S. R. and most of the countries of Europe. Declines in fertility will change this age structure in coming decades, however. Moreover, if American parents, stimulated by the advocates of lower fertility or by their own personal reasons or both, reduce further their childbearing ambitions, then the proportion of young people will be even smaller in the future. [26]

Productive work required for the prosperity of the national economy falls increasingly upon the middle class, which must help provide for those who can no longer provide for themselves. Two new factors of far-reaching importance have entered the picture in recent years. One is the impact of advancing technology upon manpower requirements; the other is the expanding role of federal government in providing support not only for the aged but for all those who have difficulty in adjusting to new conditions. Whatever influence these and related factors will have in the future, many middle-class families, whose rising income and leisure have already contributed to a declining birth rate, may feel that the greater their financial obligations, the smaller the number of children they can afford.

DECLINE IN BIRTH RATE

The decline in population growth, history shows, marks the beginning of a phase that often ends in failure to create new opportunity and new wealth. If constant, the declining birth rate would mark the long-range decline of the nation. Growing prosperity and better educational opportunity would have a pronounced effect upon the birth rate.

Surveys made earlier in the century in New York City, St. Louis, Bridgeport, Connecticut, and other cities showed that children with an I.Q. of 150 or better came from families averaging 2.2 children. As the I.Q. dropped to 110, the average number of children per family rose to 3.5. And where the I.Q. fell below 60, the average number of children reached nearly six.[27]

Studies made at about the same time in other countries showed similar findings. In England and Wales, information was obtained on the number of children per 100 married couples, with the husband under 55 years of age. Teachers, ministers, authors, and physicians had the smallest number of children, between 95 and 104; policemen and postmen, between 153 and 159; dock laborers, barmen, miners, between 231 and 259; general laborers, who are near the bottom of the economic scale, had 438 children, far outranking the nearest group. [28]

The decline in the birth rate used to be a serious problem in countries such as France. Today, it is overshadowed by: (1) the tide of world affairs including the advance of science and engineering; and (2) the population explosion in the newly developing countries which out-distances any reappearing rise in the birth rate of the developed countries.

However, the lessons of the past should not be allowed to melt away in the heat of future perils. Past studies seem to support the theory that, in terms of the individual family, a large number of children is perhaps the single greatest obstacle to the attainment of material security. But seen collectively, in terms of community and nation, a large number of children per family is a most important, in fact, indispensable requirement for the growth of population and, through it, the creation of opportunity for the growth of the nation.

Seen over a period of ten or fifteen years, a large number of children are a heavy financial and economic burden upon the average family. Seen against the background of decades and centuries, a high birth rate is the necessary foundation upon which cities, states, and nations attain positions of wealth, power, and influence.

That was the way people used to think about family and children. But seen in the changing perspective of the present and the near future, opinions about population growth are also likely to change. Quoting Dr. Herman P. Miller, Chief, Population Division, Bureau of the Census:

> Much of the discussion to date regarding the control of pollution and other social problems such as jammed highways and overcrowded schools and recreation areas has focused on reduction of population growth. I have no quarrel with this view. There is no clearly good reason why our population should continue to grow, and there appear to be many gains that could be derived from a reduction of growth. It would be easier to deal with pollution and with many of the other problems which are reducing the quality of our lives if our population grew more slowly or not at all. [29]

The late Professor Quincy Wright wrote in a special paper:

> A population policy for mankind suggests an over-all control in accord with a generally accepted plan. By such a plan, the growth rate of the total human population would be regulated so as not to exceed the pace of production of the necessities and amenities of human life, thus assuring a rising level of living for all. This over-all growth rate would be distributed by the plan among various groups permitting those which the plan considered most desirable, to increase at a more than average rate, while those considered less desirable would be permitted to remain stable or increase at a lower than average rate, and those considered positively undesirable would be eliminated, as the gardener pulls up weeds from his garden.

19

> It is obvious that such over-all control of both the whole and the parts would run against generally accepted ethical and legal concepts of the sacredness of human life, the equality of man, the freedom of religious, cultural, national and racial groups, and the independence of nations in exercising their domestic jurisdictions. Although differential rates of population growth are actually occurring among human groups, no universal authority could determine that the white race should gradually supersede the darker races or vice versa; that industrial cultures should supersede agrarian or pastoral; that English-speaking peoples should gradually supersede French, Russian, Spanish, Chinese or Arabic-speaking people; that Catholics should increase more rapidly than Protestants; Christians more rapidly than Moslems, Hindus, Jews or Buddhists; that adherents of free democracy should increase more rapidly than communists; or that the population of the United States should increase more rapidly than that of China, Russia, Germany or Japan.

While a consensus may develop that the total human population should be kept within the world's capacity, under existing technology, to maintain a high and increasing standard of living, it is unlikely that a consensus will emerge on the optimum relative size of the various segments of that population whether defined in geographic, racial, linguistic, cultural, religious, ideological, political or other terms. Each population group wants to survive and is not likely to agree that it should be superseded suddenly or gradually by rival population groups.

These considerations make it clear that it will be extremely difficult to formulate a population policy for mankind to guide the various groups composing the human family. [30]

SUMMARY

People create opportunity in two ways. One is a deliberate, natural, almost routine process in which people congregate in places where they develop community life, and through a high birth rate, prospering cities. The other is a dynamic process, although it is not always intended as such and its consequences are rarely foreseen.

The cycle of new opportunity leads from the congregation of people to the building of towns and cities, the development of commerce and industry, the continued growth of population, the production of greater wealth, the rivalry of competing power groups, and eventually to a basic change in the political climate, the economic pattern, and the controlling class.

Whenever these developments have occurred, they have had far-reaching consequences upon human affairs, especially in the last two centuries. The genius of discovery and invention changed the face of the world; it made the oceans shrink and produced scores of new countries. For the first time in history, there could be global prosperity as well as global depression. For the first time, there could be not one world war, but two. There could be two opposing social philosophies sweeping all nations. The cultural impact was no less powerful than the economic drive. And the political impact was marked by a flood of revolutions in Europe and the rest of the world.

History shows that politicians have gained from the growth of towns and cities; business men, from the development of commerce and industry; entrepreneurs, investors, and speculators, from the expansion of communication and transportation; discoverers and inventors, from the rapidly rising demand for more goods, refined products, new and better services; financiers, from the need to underwrite the vast number of new projects initiated in every field of human endeavor; artists, from the spread of cultural activity and growing interest in the arts. Millions of other persons have derived substantial benefit from the vast developments throughout the world which found their original stimulus in the growth of population and the emergence of towns and cities.

But what have the people gained in terms of equal opportunity, lasting security, and basic human dignity?

CHAPTER
TWO

THE
PEOPLE
AS
INSTRUMENTS
OF
EXPLOITATION

Do the people benefit from expanding opportunity? Do they respond when opportunity knocks? Do they protest when it is denied? Do they take an interest and participate in political developments that accompany the expansion of economic opportunity? What attitude do they take toward those who exploit that opportunity? Briefly, what is the role of the people in the stages that mark the growth of the organized society?

In the long-range perspective of history, the answer to these and related questions is mostly negative. Some of the people have benefited from expanding oportunity, but much of the world's population has lived in poverty and economic dependence throughout history; and it is living so today. If the people in general had benefited from expanding opportunity or been rewarded for their part in creating that opportunity, surely some evidence would be apparent in today's world population. What hopes may have arisen in the past have not been realized.

It may be argued that the foregoing interpretation is incorrect. Examples of poverty can be balanced by examples of prosperity, even affluence. If the people have often been frustrated, how are we to explain the progress of cities, states, nations; the advance of civilization; rising standards of living in many countries—none of which would have been likely without the economic improvement of a substantial part of the population?

Yet, if we attribute rising standards of living and the advance of civilization to the people, how could we explain the fact that, throughout history, most of the people have been denied economic security?

One answer may be that the prosperity of a country and the welfare of its population are not synonymous. Substantial numbers of people have enjoyed a degree of economic security at some time in some countries—in ancient Phoenicia, Egypt, Carthage, Athens, Rome; in medieval Italy, Holland, Spain; in modern France, Germany, Japan, England, and the United States. However, the prosperity of city, state, or nation, which advanced civilization and raised the standard of living, was rarely built upon the economic security of the majority—let alone of all of its population. The great majority of the world population has almost always lived from hand to mouth, hoping and praying for better times.

24

THE PEOPLE GROW FROM
STRONG TO WEAK

It has been pointed out that at many times in history, far from being exploited, the people have shown themselves to be strong and independent.(This situation is found particularly at the beginning of the political collective.) But the people do not remain strong and independent.

The Israelites who, in the eleventh century BC, set out to conquer Canaan, were bold and tough. They crossed the Jordan and stormed the walls of Jericho. But they did not remain free and bold. Gradually they became peasants, tilling the soil and hugging their parcel. As the people slowly assimilated and intermarried, they lost their proud, martial qualities.[1]   By the eighth century BC, the state of Israel was deteriorating. Peasants were forced to yield the soil to the landed gentry. Young people flocked to the cities. Idle rich thought up new ways of exploiting the people. Misery was widespread and despair prevailed.[2]

Ancient Rome is another example. In its early history, the plebeians were peasants and artisans. Hard, stubborn, proud, they made things difficult for the political leadership. Not until the end of the second century BC, or about six hundred years after the founding of Rome, did the patricians gain the upper hand. During the intervening centuries, the plebeians not only stood up to the patricians but added to their political rights.[3]

The people of Rome did not remain hard, proud, and independent. After the Punic Wars, the returning soldiers who filled the capital were unfit for any occupation but looting and killing. Thousands of captured slaves replaced free labor, upsetting wage and working standards. The proletariat of Rome was an idle, rapacious rabble, dominating the popular assemblies. It set up and overthrew office-holders, selling its franchise for political favors. The citizen's army was replaced by mercenary soldiers. Politicians raised ex-slaves to citizens, entertained them with bread, wine, and circus games. One-third of Rome's population, about 300,000, received their daily dole of corn. Corruption was common, bribery the rule.[4]

Aside from the Church, the early medieval era (between the sixth and ninth centuries AD) knew no greater power than that of the Franks. With the death of its founder, Clovis, the period of conquest and territorial expansion passed its peak. The real heroes of that period were the people. They served of their own free will, paid their own way, brought their own arms, did their won looting and plundering, fought on their own initiative, and often made their own laws.[5]

The Franks did not remain free and independent either. Of the simple freemen, the stronger and more resourceful rose to petty nobility; the weaker sank to serfdom. Under Charlemagne, two hundred years after Clovis, the people still constituted the army, but it was a different army. Every able-bodied man not cleric or serf was bound to take up arms. Every year, months before the military campaign got under way, the "Heerbann" was proclaimed throughout the land. Called away from their acres in spring and summer, peasants neglected the harvest. Lower classes became impoverished. Freemen were driven to serfdom. The day came when men would rather be serfs than soldiers—they would rather stay home.[6]

American history follows the same pattern. The original pioneers were a hardy group; they had to be in order to survive, let alone to conquer a new land. Americans did not remain strong, stubborn, and independent, as the early settlers had been. In seventeenth- and eighteenth-century America, the pioneer made his own church, fought his own battles, governed his own affairs; no one could tell him how to earn his livelihood. Modern Americans often prefer security to opportunity. Whereas the pioneers had no one to rely upon but themselves, modern Americans increasingly rely upon others—government leaders, management leaders, and labor leaders.

In twentieth-century America, it may be argued, people still have much to say in the political arena. Even if issues are not always clearly understood, people decide by their vote who should be elected. By voluntarily limiting their freedom, they make democracy possible. They decide which leaders they want to elect, which institutions they want to support, which goods and services they want to buy.

In a functional sense, all this is true. Americans go to the polls, patronize stores, and obey laws. But most people's affairs are not in their own hands, as they were in the pioneer period. The interests of group leadership are applied to the life of the average American with methodical precision. He is dependent upon group leadership for the terms and conditions by which he is to make his living. If he does not want to go on strike, he still must cooperate with the leadership of the union. If he does not want to retire at 65, he still must cease to work. If he does not want to see the work week reduced to 36 or 34 or even fewer hours, he still must go along.

In short, the average American is dependent upon government. For a variety of reasons (lack of education, lack of judgment, unwillingness to step out of line, he is losing control of his own actions. He does not fight whom and when he wants to. The time, place, and conditions of the fight are selected for him. Once a rugged individualist, he has become subject to the influence of powerful groups that guide his attitudes and direct his behavior. The courage of the pioneer has changed into the fear of the dependent citizen; the challenge of opportunity, into the comfort of security; tough self-reliance into complacent conformity.

In the early stages of nationhood, people have to protect themselves; no one else can or will give them protection. The American pioneer sat in front of his hut, balancing a keg of whisky on one knee, his rifle on the other. The pioneer in modern Israel builds his *kvutza* with a rifle slung over his shoulder. The settlers of ancient Rome, the Bedouins of Mohammed, the Mongols of Genghis Khan, and the followers of Bolivar were independent because they neither asked nor required outside protection.

Moreover, the pioneer depends on no one for his liveli- 27
hood. At the beginning of state or nation, human labor is by far the greatest, if not the only major asset. Economic found-ations are laid by the strong arms of the pioneer, by his willingness to forego an easier life somewhere else, and by his faith in a promising future for himself, his family, and his new land.

Finally, since these people see to their own protection, support themselves, create their own opportunity, there is no need for government to come to their help—and there is no taste for such aid on the part of the pioneer.

The factors that make the people strong are the necessity to shift for themselves and the opportunity to advance on their own initiative and determination. People change when they find out they do not have to be strong and independent to be employed by someone else. In fact, strength and boldness may be a disadvantage. The absence of necessity and the presence of ready security tend to make the people dependent.[7]

THE PEOPLE LACK BROADER INTERESTS

The failure of the people to benefit from expanding opportunity can be attributed to two conditions: their lack of sustained interest in the affairs of the body politic and their lack of ability to take advantage of opportunity. The basic interests of the people are limited to physical survival. As was pointed out earlier, one principal characteristic of the people is their almost complete absorption in the task of making a living. It is only natural then that their main interest would be in things that bear upon their own survival and that of their families: job, home, farm, food; protection against the cost of sickness, against rising prices, and against insecurity.

No matter how strong, industrious, and independent, the people by themselves have never organized at a higher level than that of plain economic need, simple religious ritual, uncomplicated military action, and similar activities. If they had, they would have acted as the people have never acted before; they would have acted as leaders.

History tells of many instances where the people conquered foreign soil, expanded their possessions, and held them against their enemies. History also tells many an epic story of the heroism of the people, their pride, gallantry, industry, humility, tenacity, and naked courage. It will be difficult, however, to find instances where the people engaged in a feat of arms or a successful struggle with the soil to a point where the survival of the group was secured through political organization. That requires leadership.

The people of the thirteen colonies knew how to shoot, to build houses, and to force the virgin land to yield a good crop. But it took others to design the political pattern, to construct the framework of the nation, and to shape a constitution to safeguard civil rights and protect private property.

The pattern applies to smaller political groups. Venice, whose beginnings were poor, grew to financial, commercial, and political predominance in the medieval world. Driven upon the shoals of the deserted island by the marauding

Magyars, the first Venetians knew how to build huts and how to perfect weaving and other crafts.[8] But they were unable to do more than provide for their own needs. It took leadership to build a city, to organize trade, to launch, equip, and lead into battle a fleet of men-of-war.

To produce a city, state, or nation requires the ability to advance a group from the simple pattern to the complex system. People are not equipped to develop knowledge, interest, determination, responsibility, let alone leadership, to the degree necessary for a more complex society. If this was true in the past, it is doubly true in the modern age which is complicated enormously by the advance of science and technology. The mechanics of the modern economy, the workings of modern government, the intricacies of foreign affairs, the organization of labor, and the technique of mass-psychology are so involved, their effects so far-reaching, their ramifications so extensive that the specialist can do no more than cover a limited area, and the leader can do no more than decide which specialist to call on in which eventuality.

It is in the historical record that in matters of war and foreign policy, the voice of the people is not a controlling factor. Says Walter Millis, speaking of recent United States history:

29

> Vice President Nixon had condemned the publication of the fact that 80 per cent of the State Department mail had been running against the Quemoy policy. Decisions in foreign policy, he said, should not be made "on the basis of opinion polls"; foreign policy simply cannot be founded on indications as to "what the people will support in the light of the minimum and often misleading information available to them.". . .

> But even if government were at greater pains than it is to see that the people get a maximum of non-misleading information, it is doubtful that Mr. Nixon or any other thoughtful person could accept "what the people will support" as a valid basis for foreign policy decisions. In our tradition, the people are sovereign, and it is considered an essential of political liberty that all citizens have a voice in the great decisions which govern their destiny. But in the examples cited, all the protagonists—Cleveland, Olney, Eisenhower and Nixon—eliminate the people as a controlling factor in matters of war and foreign policy, leaving the President as a dictator whose lonely word must, in the last analysis, decide.[9]

POLITICAL INDIFFERENCE

Lack of interest, added to lack of knowledge and ability, creates opportunity for others to use the people for their own ends. Indifference accentuates dependence. Exploiting that dependence may be selfish interests, as in the case of a tyrant, despot, or dictator; or they may be unselfish interests, as in the case of a liberal leader or a religious group. The interests may be for or against democracy; for or against collectivism; for or against nation, church, labor union, private enterprise, racial minorities, and other groups or institutions.

Thus, the people become the willing though often unwitting instrument of purposes that may be of no personal interest to them. Mostly, they are used in the interest of the existing order, but not infrequently they are called upon by agitators, propagandists, prophets, poets, and intellectuals to help bring about a new order. In either case, the people are used to exploit the leader's opportunities: their votes are used to put or to keep a political party or leader in power; their military service to fight or to prevent a war; their devotion and sacrifice to cultivate a religion; their support to control a labor union; their citizenship to rule a nation. They are asked to sacrifice for the common cause, giving up their individual rights and prerogatives in the process.

History seems clear on one point: it is not the people who make the revolution; they barely support it. Sometimes they hinder, even resist it. Often they have to be forced to accept changes obviously beneficial to them. The people had to be forced to accept the House of Burgesses; attendance was compulsory for 83 years, which was apparently the only way to keep it alive. People had to be forced to accept the absolute rule of the Crown. The rise of feudalism and, before that, the ascendancy of the medieval Church brought benefits to the people. Yet both institutions had to be forced upon them.

The people did not want Cromwell; they would have been content with Charles I. When Charles II returned to the throne in his stead, they were satisfied, too. They were willing to accept the House of Parliament on a hereditary basis.

Political indifference is fostered by the absence of any real desire for change. If their physical needs are satisfied, the people are generally glad, or at least willing, to accept existing conditions. As Sir Arthur Haselrig said in the seventeenth century:

> They care not what government they live under,
> so they may plow and go to market.[10]

This may be a sad remark from the perspective of political interest and social responsibility, but not from the point of view of a man who must provide a living for his family.

PASSIVE ROLE IN REVOLUTIONS

The minor role that the people play in the active phases of a revolution is born out by statistics. The New Model Army of the English Revolution began with a membership of 22,000, and never, even in its most active days, reached more than 40,000, or about one per cent of the population. [11]

What is sometimes called a sense of loyalty may actually be indifference. During the English Revolution, with the conflict between Puritans and Catholics, between Parliament and Charles I raging in full fury, the people were innocent bystanders. Political rights, religious issues, economic opportunities meant little compared with loyalty to the king. [12]

The American Revolution was not welcomed by the people. Reportedly, it was actively engineered, supported, and fought by less than 10 per cent of the population. [13] Many years later, independence for the white and later for the colored people were unwelcome war measures. [14]

The French Revolution derived its principal strength from the Jacobin clubs, whose membership consisted of the more prosperous citizens. At the peak of their power, the Jacobins constituted between 2 and 3 per cent of the population of about 20,000,000. [15]

31

The people's general indifference toward political issues permits them only a minor temporary role in revolutionary efforts. As soon as the revolution is ended, the traditional apathy takes over. At the high point of the French Revolution, in 1789, every physically able citizen went to the polls. Four years later, when much of the revolutionary fervor had worn off, in many districts less than one-tenth of the qualified voters made use of the franchise.[16,17,18] The same apathy that characterized people's attitude toward political issues throughout history is present in the contemporary period.

In the Russian Revolution, the Bolsheviks never represented more than one per cent of a population of well over one hundred million.[19] Lenin had firm opinions on the part the people might be expected to play in the planned revolution. He did not count on the peasants, who had been of little help in the uprising of 1905. Only bribe, he was convinced, could persuade them to support the Bolshevik cause. To the peasants he promised land; to the workers, factories. He knew, along with Rosa Luxemburg and other leaders, that these could never be fulfilled. Ownership of land would create a bourgeoisie and ownership of the factories would encourage trade unions. Neither would promote communism; on the contrary, they would oppose it. Indifferent to the revolution, the people wanted peace, bread, and work. Lenin the propagandist made the necessary concessions. Lenin the dictator cancelled those that proved undesirable.[20]

Although the planners of the Russian Revolution had their differences of opinion, they apparently agreed on the role of the people. At the Second Conference of the Revolutionary and Social Democratic Parties in 1903, the majority of the delegates, mostly Bolsheviks, voted for Lenin's proposal, to wit: that it is preposterous to believe that the masses can be converted to socialism; that the only promising strategy was the organization of small, compact fighting units of secretly chosen, carefully trained technicians. The people were to be left out of the movement's more active phases.[21]

Even the promise of a share in the profits of the state-controlled economy (or, as the early Nazis promised, transfer of the large department stores to the ownership of the people) is motivated not so much by any ambitious desire on the part of the people for entrepreneurial opportunity as by the desire of their leaders to see the capitalists eliminated and their properties confiscated.

One reason why the people play a minor part in revolutionary struggles may be found in the fact that the philosophy of the revolutionary leaders is sometimes contradictory. They profess grandiose aims at economic reorganization and the redistribution of wealth. The people do not seem to be interested in wealth. Therefore, instead of wealth, revolutionary leaders promise land, food, work, housing, free education, social security, and other benefits. The emphasis is on security rather than on opportunity.

Nor do the people begrudge wealth, of which they have scarce knowledge. While they are acquainted with some of the manifestations of wealth, such as large estates, stables, winter gardens, jewelry, furs, yachts, and opera boxes, they know little of its productive character. If the people were conscious of wealth as a highly creative force of extraordinary power, they would no longer classify as "the people." They would display insight, larger interests, and aspirations extending far beyond the physical needs of today and tomorrow.

At one point in the historical development of the collective—when the pressure of physical needs becomes extreme—the people shake off their political indifference. Through the ages, the people have risen in protest against desperate conditions. At the same time, their failure to organize resistance or to take effective action to follow up that resistance underlines their lack of ability to take advantage of opportunity.

33

RIOTS

In ancient Greece, about the ninth century BC, the peasants lived in utter poverty. They fell into debt, lost their land to the nobles, became day laborers, even sold themselves into slavery. There were scattered uprisings but no organized resistance.[22]

In the eighth century BC, great poverty lay upon Israel. The peasants lost the land to the gentry; the people were forced to till the soil in virtual slavery; starvation was widespread. Again, there were occasional uprisings but no organized resistance against ruthless exploitation. [23]

Perhaps the greatest misery that the people in many parts of France ever suffered occurred between 1660 and 1670. Violent disorders broke out in Poitou, Bourges, Bordeaux, Lyons, and many other cities. Butchers rebelled, paupers and beggars rioted, women demonstrated. The government, not as weak and corrupt as it would be a century later, acted promptly. Leaders among the rioters were hanged, others were imprisoned; the people's heavy burden was made a little heavier. There was no organized resistance. [24]

In seventeenth-century England, while artisans, merchants, the gentry, and the Church possessed power and wealth, the lower classes in the cities suffered greatly. They were joined in their protestations by thousands of farm laborers who had been deprived of their livelihood when Henry VIII seized large tracts of land for his sheep to graze. There was much discontent but there was no organized resistance. [25]

These "riots" have in common not only the people's violent protests against extreme exploitation and abuse but also the failure of their efforts to obtain a measure of relief. And in all cases the reason was the same: lack of organization and leadership.

REBELLIONS

History has many examples of uprisings on the next higher level. These uprisings, or "rebellions," combine conditions of severe economic hardship with organization and leadership. Starting from the same general premise as riots, rebellions are of weightier consequence. They are usually of greater scope, involve larger numbers of people, and often try to get at the cause of economic distress. If they fail in spite of these advantages, it is due to a common fault: they fail to gain the support of some of the ruling powers.

Spartacus, the gladiator who sought to free the slaves from Roman tyranny, was a competent leader. His cause was important and enjoyed wide support. His 90,000 slave-followers defeated two Roman armies. Yet, in the end, Spartacus lost. He never gained the support of some of the ruling powers.

In fourteenth-century England, Wat Tyler led the rebellion of rural laborers and the lower class of craftsmen. Aided by good leadership and effective organization (and not a little by fire, murder, and treachery), his movement carried to the throne of fourteen-year-old Richard II. Lacking the support of some of the vested interests, his rebellion collapsed.

The German Peasant Wars are a good example of the difference between rebellion and revolution. The peasant leaders thought they could rely on the support of Martin Luther and the princes; a revolution seemed to build up. After encouraging the peasants to revolt, Luther apparently changed his mind. He advised the princes to show the peasants no mercy, the latter paying for their folly with 50,000 lives. That was the end of the rebellion. [26,27]

REVOLUTIONS

The next level of uprisings, the "revolutions," combines conditions of severe economic hardship with leadership and organization, plus the support of some of the ruling powers. This opposition movement is the most important because, on a substantial scale, it is the only successful one. The support of some of the ruling interests is apparently indispensable to the success of an uprising. The formula seems to be confirmed by history, even in circumstances where an outside factor of major importance, like a disastrous war, imposes abnormal conditions. In that case, a revolution may succeeed without substantial support on the part of any of the ruling powers, as in the Russian uprisings of 1917. But unless military or other major interests eventually join the rebellious forces, the revolutionary party is not likely to prevail for long.

Even a rebellion that has developed far into revolutionary significance will collapse when some of the ruling interests withdraw their support. A case in point is the movement of Catiline which was well organized and well led. With the backing of Caesar and Crassus, it had a good chance to succeed as a full-scale revolution. Having achieved their objective of diverting the movement to oppose the senatorial party rather than the propertied class, Caesar and Crassus abandoned Catiline's cause. It soon collapsed. [28]

In a nobler cause, another Roman failed no less decisively. Two generations before Catiline, the popular movement of Tiberius Gracchus was successful as long as it was backed by the big money party: the equites. When the reforms in which they were interested had been enacted, the equites withdrew, marking the doom of Gracchus' movement.

The French Revolution was preceded by nearly a century of localized riots. When organized and properly led, the riots became a rebellion. But only when the *tiers*, the money party, left the Crown and joined the two other estates, did the rebellion become a revolution. [29]

After the First World War, Germany was the scene of many major rebellions. Being in a strong position after the armistice, the Communists lost control quickly when the important economic interests lined up against them. The subsequent coalition of Social-Democrats, the Catholic Center, and other parties was successful as long as it had the support of a substantial part of the economic interests. However, when they did not get either enough business for themselves or the harsh treatment they felt the Communists deserved, these interests swung their support to the Nazi rebellion, which promised huge arms contracts on the one side and ruthless persecution of Communists on the other. With the backing of heavy industry and high finance, the rebellion became a full-fledged revolution.

In the United States, there were riots before there was a revolution—riots over taxes, riots over land titles, riots over good timber being reserved by the Crown for shipbuilding, riots over the actions of English captains in seizing Americans for the Royal Navy, riots over the stamp tax, riots over the Molasses Act, riots over military service, riots over the Townsend Acts.[30] Few of these riots brought even temporary relief. Success came only when some of the more important interests gave purpose, direction, and leadership to the scattered movement. With their backing, the many little causes became one big cause. Riots grew into rebellions and eventually into a full-scale revolution.

Pre-revolutionary promises differ sharply from post-revolutionary realities. Revolution has brought the people new social institutions (Soviet Russia), new forms of government (England), greater political rights (ancient Rome), and different class concepts (France). It has never relieved the people of their concern over their physical needs, their fears of the future, or their need for protection. It has never changed the relationship between the people and their leaders, never lessened the people's dependence upon the leaders for their livelihood.

Even when the people initially share in the fruits of the revolution, they find themselves on the losing side as soon as the new powers feel secure in the saddle. The communal revolution in medieval Europe is an example.

Will Durant describes the rise of new classes to economic and political power during the economic revolution of the twelfth and thirteenth centuries. The feudal baron or bishop in the ninth and tenth centuries still ruled the towns of central Europe, but the growing population became increasingly commercial and began to rebel against feudal tolls and controls. Towards the end of the eleventh century, the merchant leaders began to demand for the towns charters of communal freedom from the feudal overlords. The struggle continued for a century.

By the end of the twelfth century, the communal revolution had succeeded in Western Europe. Feudal tolls were reduced or abolished, and ecclesiastical rights severely limited. But as soon as the mercantile bourgeoisie dominated the municipal and economic life, it turned against the people. In many cities it eliminated the poor from assemblies and offices. It oppressed the manual worker and the peasant, monopolized the profits of commerce, and heavily taxed the community. It tried to suppress artisan associations and refused them the right to strike under penalty of exile or death.

37

Its regulations of prices and wages were extremely detrimental to the working class. The defeat of the feudal lords was a victory chiefly for the new mercantile class. [31]

SIGNIFICANCE

By emphasizing the plight of the people I do not mean to imply that the exploitation of their dependence was an *occasional* policy. The basic function of the people in the human society has never fundamentally changed; their economic and political dependence has been a cornerstone in society's evolution. Contrary to popular belief, the people do not derive lasting economic security or political freedom from new opportunity. They do not possess the initiative and determination required to take advantage of opportunity, and they lack the interest without which even the best opportunity is purposeless.

I would similarly dispute other beliefs: specifically, that the people can be relied on to bring about the things or conditions they want; that the people, if correctly informed, will find their own way; that the principles and policies of city, state, nation, church, labor union, or other groups are determined by the people; and that the voice and the judgment of the people cannot be controlled.

These and similar beliefs have never been confirmed by history—on the contrary, they have been disproved. As history tells it, people cannot and do not determine the merit of principles and policies. If they had, the principle of leadership could never have scored the unbroken string of achievements and successes that history records.

Sad as this judgment may seem, it is both necessary and true. For much too long, the people have been flattered, glorified, falsely impressed, and misled. It is the easiest way to obtain their approbation and acclaim, but such blandishments do not help the people secure freedom, security, or independence. The first step toward such help must be the recognition of the true role and character of the people in the past history of society.

In the light of historical evidence—that the people are indifferent toward major political change, that the people are not helped by revolution, that the people cannot be expected to evaluate carefully basic issues—it is obvious that those who want to better the lot of the people cannot rely on the people to help themselves. They must not assume that the people have the incentive or the interest in the later stages of the growing political collective. Nor must they rely on revolution to bring about this betterment. Revolutions are a contest of leadership. What they change is not the basic role of the people but the personalities, identities, interests, and power of leadership classes.

If this apparently unalterable principle of economic and political dependence is accepted as beyond human control, what reason is there to believe that the people can ever gain true freedom; that their lot can be improved permanently; or that they can be liberated of their fears? Why would we support revolutions? Why would we oppose socialism or capitalism, communism or democracy? Do we want the people to exchange one kind of dependence for another? Do we want to make them believe that one kind is true independence while the other is nearly slavery? And can we do all this in the name of the people everywhere and for their universal benefit?

However, instead of accepting the basic dependence of the people and the invariable defeat of all efforts to gain their freedom, one could argue that this interpretation of the people in history is wrong; that the great minds and courageous leaders of the past, who dedicated themselves to the liberation of the people, did not know how to cope with the problem; that our superior knowledge, aided by science, technology, and other achievements, gives us a completely new kind of opportunity to help the people; that our age can become better, wiser, more resourceful, and more humane than any previous age. One can cite that the miraculous attainments of the contemporary world and argue that perhaps even more miraculous attainments of the world of tomorrow will make a basic difference in the future—a difference so basic that the record of the past will lose much of its validity.

We turn then to an examination of the implications of the future.

CHAPTER
THREE

THE
PEOPLE
IN
THE
FUTURE

41

The grave problems that may arise from population growth on the one side and the great advances that may result from it on the other are considered by Teilhard de Chardin:

> From the paleolithic age onwards, and still more after the neolithic age, Man has always lived in a state of expansion; to him progress and increase have been one and the same thing. But now we see the saturation point ahead of us, and approaching at a dizzy speed. How are we to prevent this compression of Mankind on the closed surface of the planet (a thing that is good in itself, as we have seen, since it promotes social unification) from passing that critical point beyond which any increase in numbers will mean famine and suffocation? Above all, how are we to ensure that the maximum population, when it is reached, shall be composed only of elements harmonious in themselves and blended as harmoniously as possible together?[1]

WILL SCIENCE AND TECHNOLOGY
MAKE A DIFFERENCE?

If in the past population growth led to new opportunity and the rise of new nations, and if a decline in population led to diminishing opportunity and the downfall of nations, will this pattern be repeated in the future? Or can developments in science and technology be expected to bring about controls of population growth and its impact upon society?

It is impossible to say what the future will bring. So many unknown factors and intangibles are involved that future trends cannot be judged with any degree of accuracy. Notwithstanding these and other limitations, I believe it is fruitful and relevant to compare the record of the past with the anticipated development of the future and to give some thought to the long-term significance of population growth and decline. This significance is not confined to statistical data but is revealed in basic and dynamic changes that the world of tomorrow is bound to experience. With this in mind, I shall outline briefly some of the arguments pro and con with regard to this question:

> Will further developments in science and technology make a basic difference in the control of population growth and its impact upon society, thereby changing the people's traditional pattern of economic and political dependence?

ARGUMENTS PRO

In the future, basic changes in the population control can be expected. The impact of population changes will be less pronounced than in the past because they will be anticipated, calculated, and controlled. More and more people will live in scattered communities rather than in metropolitan centers. Many people will work at home as a result of widespread corporate employment made possible by refined communications and control networks. Especially in the highly developed countries, there will be expanding decentralization of industry.

In the past, fertility coincided with poverty caused by economic exploitation. These highly explosive conditions contributed to the overthrow of classes and governments and to the rise of new leaders. In the future, advancing technology will accelerate economic development, spread wealth more evenly, and reduce or eliminate poverty. Advanced nations have created a kind of prefabricated technology which allows developing countries to attain instant industrial status.

It took the United States more than fifty years to develop a textile industry; it need not take a country like Peru more than a fraction of that time to build a textile industry compatible with the needs of her domestic economy. It took the United States two score years to develop its highway system; a country like Arabia can construct its system in far less time. It took the United States many years to develop a machine tool industry; the Soviet Union was able to establish such an industry within a few Five-Year Plans. The time differential is largely explained by the fact that much of the thinking, searching, designing, probing, and experimental effort—expensive and time-consuming as it is—has been mostly completed, and the results have become available to potential users.

Future technology will provide wealth, or at least a comfortable living, for more than a select few. Birth control will be widely available as a result of expanded economic security and education. Fertility control agents may even be administered in the water supply or in food production.

Corporations may redirect social thought and action, focusing greater attention on the educational, housing, and occupational needs of the people. Continuing growth in corporate enterprise, supported by continued advances in science and technology, will bring about broader cooperation among the nations. No longer tied to any one country, global business organizations will encourage greater political unity among the peoples of the world. Instead of exploiting the less-developed countries, the great powers will extend a helping hand, as some are doing today. The effect of cooperative action on a world-wide scale will be to prevent or at least to soften the resentment and bitterness that accumulated among native populations during the colonial period. The future attitude of these people toward the industrialized nations will become more conciliatory and cooperative. The people will become increasingly free and independent.

ARGUMENTS CON

While the realization of these predictions is in the interest of the people, there are few indications that the expectations are justified. It is possible to forecast not only the opportunities of the future but also its limitations. Technology may not continue to advance. Policy analyst Franklin P. Huddle of the Congressional Research Service says, "There are both intended and unintended effects of technology, and the unintended [ones] tend to be more indeterminate, intangible, and ultimately almost infinite in scope. . . ." [2] Also, many people think man has enough technology and should turn his mind to other things. [3]

Poorly controlled technological advances bring great benefits but also cause social instability, personality problems, and environmental damage. The solutions to these adversities will probably require a reordering of values, a reshuffling of leadership, and perhaps a restructuring of society. That the results will be beneficial to the people is by no means assured.

With its powerful impact upon education, labor, management, and other branches of human activity, technological advance will reduce the number of people in the poverty class, but it will also increase the number of high-income individuals, especially of professional and managerial personnel. These positions will be the training ground for the new leadership class. The bulk of the people will not be affected nor will their traditional dependence role, even if their living standards are somewhat improved.

One of the most pronounced effects of continued technological advance will be the trend toward giant institutions. Giantism will dominate not only buildings, laboratories, machines, the means of communication and transportation, schools, libraries, arenas, concert halls, museums, and other centers of human activity, but also institutions of government, labor, industry, education, medical care, the arts, science, and many others. Caught in the vortex of such breathtaking size and complexity, the individual is likely to feel more helpless and less needed than ever before.

A statement issued at the conclusion of a conference on "Technology, Man and Nature" under the joint sponsorship of the Aspen (Colorado) Institute for Humanistic Studies and the International Association for Cultural Freedom, September 6, 1970, summarized:

> The need is not for the slower development of technology, either in advanced or in developing countries. Such a slowdown would cruelly sacrifice the interests of millions of underprivileged people whose hopes and expectations cannot begin to be met without more technology. The need is rather for more thoughtful and careful application of new technologies to prevent both long range damage to the earth and violence to human values and to foster social, economic, and cultural development. [4]

45

In the past, population pressure was mitigated by disaster, disease, and war. In the modern age, its effect is intensified by the steady gain of new knowledge in medicine and hygiene and, oddly enough, by broad social progress. More people live longer. Notwithstanding industrial decentralization, more people will want to live in modernized cities where they will expect to find better protection in case of illness, unemployment, old age, and other adversities, individual and collective.

The more technology is perfected, the greater its productivity. The constant need is not only for new consumers but for an increased capacity of present consumers. Technology cannot progress unless an expanding economy can absorb its output. In the future, technological progress will flow from the highly industrialized to the developing countries. To be similarly successful, each technological advance will require an expanding consumer demand throughout the world. Technology could play a decisive role in bringing this about: it could raise two billion underprivileged people to the level of consumers and then, heighten consumer demand to the highest possible level. So far, modern technology has done little for the vast numbers of ill-fed, ill-clad, ill-housed people in Asia, Africa, and other continents, where poverty is greatest and fertility highest.

The advance of science and technology will most certainly make a difference, says Professor Nathan Keyfitz, Department of Demography, University of California, Berkeley, but the indicated results can hardly be judged either in the favor or the interest of the people. In a special paper, Professor Keyfitz says:

> The ability of capitalism to produce material goods has been paralleled by its production of people. This latter was a "spin-off" from the early industrial system which not only survives into the present, but has attained a momentum of its own. The concern about the people-producing process as we enter the last third of the twentieth century lies especially in the fact that the people and the goods are not being produced in the same places, and disproportions in the rates are leading to unprecedented contrasts of wealth and poverty.

> This inequality in command of goods is given a strange aspect by a pathological elaboration of the 19th-century concept of nationhood, in which the poor insist on living independently, and in separate territorial units from the rich. The fantasies for which liberal romantics fought in 19th-century Greece and Italy, and conservative romantics in Germany, have now become common-sense reality to the inhabitants of Ceylon and Tanzania. The newly created large populations are framed in one or another national state, of which there are now approximately 120. If things go as badly as they may during the next 33 years, the end of the century could see about one billion rich people, mostly of European and Japanese descent, in a score of countries, facing five or more billion desperately poor, in a hundred national states. The population problem which is intimately related to the problem of development is given an especially critical turn by a decisive alteration of Western technology which took place in the middle third of the twentieth century.[5]

The basic objective of industrialism, it is pointed out, is the attainment of a profit. The usual means to this end is to

46

compete with other interests that either are operating at a profit or are planning to do so. Thus, the interest of one party runs counter to that of a competing party, since a factory or store owner will usually find it necessary to compete with other factory or store owners. The owners may wish their competitors well; but if they want to be successful, they will do all in their power to obtain more business and to make larger profits, even at the expense of their competitors.

This example does not mean that competitors cannot live in peace. Competition as a principle of human aspiration is sound and justified. But it is obvious that systems such as capitalism or socialism, which operate upon the profit motive (be it for the individual or the state), may sometimes be hard pressed to apply the principle of unselfishness for its own sake. The controlling interests are not likely to modify either the profit motive or the competitive urge because they would do harm to the foundation on which they operate. If the developing nations are to derive the benefits of technology, they will probably have to obtain them the hard way: by competition with the established interests.

Nor is there valid reason under the prevailing system to expect better relations between the nations in the future. The things that set nations apart are not the things they have in common: farms and factories, railroads, highways and airlines, schools, libraries and universities. The things that set them apart are their differences: the American way of life, the American flag and form of government, American tradition and history, American credoes and standards, American rights and interests. A nation that minimizes rather than emphasizes its contrasting features endangers its survival as a nation, as Akhenaten did in ancient Egypt, or Chamberlain in modern Britain. The nation's identity depends upon the preservation of its own clear distinctions. Obviously, the nation whose existence, let alone success, is predicated upon a basically selfish interest can hardly be expected to pursue a basically unselfish attitude toward other nations.

The principles of identity and opposition are too complex to discuss here in their full significance. If they are mentioned, it is for the purpose of pointing out that modern civilization, its culture and technique, is not likely to change the societal role people have played in the past and are playing now.

Therefore it may be assumed that the future effect of population growth and decline will follow the historical pattern. It will create new opportunity, new wealth, new forms of government, new ways of living. But rather than mitigate, it may intensify conflict. Rather than unify human society, it may create sharper dissension among its segments. Some countries and continents will have an acute problem of population growth sooner than others. Europe has had a population problem for a long time; it has yet to find a lasting solution.

THE SHORT-TERM FUTURE OF EUROPE

To the first settlers in America, the continent was undeveloped and sparsely settled. The Spanish, French, Dutch, and English arrivals forced the native population into narrow confines where they could not stand in the way of economic expansion. Although the process was repeated in other colonial ventures by European powers, it proved unworkable in Europe. Germany and Italy may serve as examples.

The population pressure in Germany and Italy led to considerable economic expansion, but a lack of space prevented these countries from solving their population problem. They could not apply the continental pattern of the United States or the empire pattern of Great Britain. The Germans attempted to gain control of the European continent; the Italians, to build a Mediterranean empire. Both met with defeat because, unlike the Americans and the British, their attempts ran into powerful well-organized resistance.

The two major European powers were defeated, but the underlying problem was not eliminated. The causes of war remain. Defeat is survived by continuing population pressure. The old ambitions are alive, awaiting tomorrow's opportunity. New leaders will design new plans and new means of gain and conquest. For a time, the pressures in any one country may be held in check by the pressures arising from still larger, still more rapidly growing populations, as the Japanese may be checked by the Chinese, the Germans by the Russians. In the end, population pressure will make its own solution.

The future of Europe is likely to be decided by the economic opportunities engendered by that pressure. Regardless of his methods, Bismarck showed sound reasoning when he founded the German Reich. The new industrialism gave Germany a predominant position on the continent. Improved methods of transportation enhanced the natural advantages of her central location. Increasing population along with new economic opportunities underlined the advantages of concentration everywhere—in population through urban expansion, in industry through the development of cartels, and in politics through federation of the provinces. What Napoleon could not accomplish sixty and seventy years before, nor Frederick the Great a hundred years before, Bismarck was able to realize, helped by a growing population and new economic opportunity.

The Second World War left Europe divided into two camps. Population pressure influenced developments in East as well as West Europe for many years. However, its impact upon technological advance has been most pronounced in the West. The countries behind the Iron Curtain, except the industrial areas of Poland and Czechoslovakia, are removed from the dynamic industrial center of Europe which stretches from lower Scandinavia to upper Italy, and from (pre-Second World War) southeast Germany to central France.

In order to realize the full potential of this area, the nations of *Mittel-Europa* must create greater economic opportunity by eliminating political barriers, tariffs, and other obstacles. They must build among themselves the understanding and cooperation needed to devise new methods of manufacturing and marketing, that is, the means of producing new wealth. The intellectual beginnings of such a development were seen some thirty years ago in the Pan-Europe movement of Count Coudenhove-Kalergi; the physical beginnings of it are seen in the Five-Power Pact of 1956 for economic cooperation, which has since expanded into the Common Market.

In this way, population pressure, far from being relieved, continues toward the creation of ever greater economic opportunity. If that pressure had been siphoned off in past decades to other parts of the world, the results might have been similar to the British experience. During the last two centuries, British influx of population, administration, investment, industrial and commercial enterprise, into colonial territories made them increasingly independent of the mother country; this new independence was largely a result of the opportunities created by population growth.

Continued population pressure has caused continued technological advance in the countries of Europe's dynamic economic center. In order to live, these countries must compete. Not strong enough by themselves, they must eventually unite—not primarily to fulfill some Pan-European scheme, nationalistic idea, racial dream, or political vision, but to create new wealth and power on a large scale. In order to compete with the United States and the Soviet Union, not to mention future power blocs, the countries of *Mittel-Europa* eventually will have to unite in a well-integrated and highly competitive economy on a continental scale. This union is the most likely long-term effect of the pressures created by several hundred million people living in this dynamic center, and of the vast economic opportunities of which they are the principal ingredient.

THE LONG-TERM FUTURE OF THE PEOPLE IN DEVELOPING COUNTRIES

The economic effect of population growth is a new problem in the developing countries. Confucians and Buddhists in China, Hindus in India, Moslems reaching from the rim of the Mediterranean south to Dark Africa, and Roman Catholics in Latin America are all largely strangers to urban living, to science and technology, to industrialism, and to the complex system of wealth-creation. Whatever acquaintance they may have with these things is less of their own making than it is the result of foreign initiative and enterprise.

While these people may not have yet experienced the economic effect of population growth, they have already demonstrated its power—although not directly in their own interest and only partly to their own advantage. With the growing impact of Western technology and the subsequent increase in population, the age-old trend, leading from fertility to urban development, invention, industrialism, wealth-creation, and eventually to the overthrow of class systems and governmental hierarchies, is beginning to assert itself.

The People's Republic of China, with a still-growing population estimated between 700 and 800 million, is a prime example of this trend. The entire country is alive with hard, vigorous, dynamic activity in which everyone is a participant —peasant, worker, professional, technician, student, and teacher. No one has time to stop, to relax, to think. The challenge is: Produce and Perform! In its spirit of devotion and sacrifice to the cause, and in its faith, courage, and self-reliance, China is today where the United States was in its pioneer days more than a century ago. But in terms of applied science and technology, China is marching ahead of today, as manifested in its urban development, its industrial design, its educational and cultural program, its inventive genius tested over five millennia, and its restructuring of society—all laid out in gigantic dimensions. In this vast enterprise, the people are playing the most important role. But what their role will be when the pioneering task is completed in the not too distant future is likely to be determined by the very dynamism that generated their initial endeavor.

In the history of India, a large population was the chief factor blocking opportunity. Labor was so abundant that there was no need of more efficient tools for the creation of greater wealth. Hence, there was little new opportunity. This situation is changing. The people of India are rapidly learning highway construction, modern farming methods, hygiene, and the manufacture of textiles and other products. The resignation of poverty is yielding to the vision of material things. From the time Robert Clive set foot on India's soil, her vast population contributed materially to the establishment and growth of the British Empire. Now, that same population is the greatest single factor in the awakening national consciousness and in the making of an independent economy.

The considerable tangible riches of the Arab world cannot compare with the potential wealth it possesses in its people. Historical experience indicates that this potential wealth will prove to be immeasurably greater than all the oil, cotton, spices, and other products that foreign powers have been and still are exacting from the Arab world. As the possibilities of modern technology dawn upon the Arab leaders, and as the new opportunities assume more concrete forms, as are evident in modern Israel, growing national pride will spur new economic development. The basic factor in the evolution of an independent Arab economy and its new opportunities will be continued fertility, that is, a large and growing population.

In a similar way, dynamic opportunities engendered by rapid population increases are likely to determine the future of Africa. Valued today for its copper, ivory, diamonds, and the vast resources of every kind of vegetation, Africa may derive its future importance from the potential wealth represented by the mighty reservoir of its native population.

Today, the value of Central and South America is calculated in terms of coffee, cocoa, sugar, cotton, bauxite, bananas, rubber, oil, tin, and many other products. Tomorrow, their large and growing populations will turn the uses of modern technology to their own advantage, helped not a little by the surge of awakening national pride.

The progression from population growth to economic, political, and cultural advance has become accelerated in recent times. It has also changed its sequence. Now, the effect of population growth may show up first in the overthrow of governments, as in Morocco, Egypt, Iran, Iraq, and other parts of Asia and Africa. In this sequence, one misses the interim phase of technical evolution which was characteristic of European and American economic development. Actually, this episode has not been skipped; it has been executed by foreign rather than native enterprise, as seen in the foreign-controlled development of railroads, construction, mining, oil, sugar, rubber, and other industries and plantations. Native enterprise needs time to mature before it is able to take charge of the development. In some countries, the time has come; in others, it is near at hand; in still others, it is in the maturing stage.

Confucians, Moslems, Hindus, and Latin Americans will begin to shape the destinies of their countries as soon as they have learned the historical lesson, to wit: before the people can make the full impact of their numbers felt, they must progress from the dispersed to the concentrated form of group living. Europe learned by trial and error; it took over a thousand years. Copying much of the collective pattern of living, by working, trading, and communicating with the European experience, the United States required less than two centuries to develop a highly refined technical and cultural society. Copying still more extensively from modern America, Indians, Arabs, Moslems, Negroes, and Latin Americans will require less than a century, perhaps much less.

SIGNIFICANCE

These observations indicate that the impact of advancing   53
science and technology will indeed make a difference in the future. But it is not likely to make a basic difference in the societal roles and relationships of the people, or in the forces determining those roles. Changes will occur. Basic values will not change, but individual values will replace collective values; individuality will supplant conformity. Basic relationships will remain, but new forms of relationship will develop, for example, that of the natural to the social scientist, or of the American to the Russian or Chinese cosmonaut. Basic ideas will endure but a large selection of new ideas making for greater or better productivity, for an easier or richer life, or whatever the improvement may be will spring up. The traditional role of the people in society will be preserved but the methods of their exploitation will be refined through new devices of communication and information, through new techniques of propaganda and thought suggestion, and through other means of more or less subtle design.

Another aspect might be borne in mind. Under existing societal relationships, the future role of the people should not be considered merely a consequence of technological impact. I have so far discussed only the people, but their role can hardly be judged in its full significance unless the role of those who help determine it is taken into consideration.

The role of outstanding persons in every field of endeavor emphasizes the fact that the few, to lead, must have the many, to follow. The advocates of freedom found their opportunity only when the oppressed or dissatisfied people were ready to follow them: the Roman slaves followed Spartacus; the industrial workers, Lenin; the American people, Franklin D. Roosevelt. The great exploiters found their opportunity in similar circumstances: the Romans followed Caesar; the Mongols, the Great Khan; the French, Napoieon; the Germans, Hitler. In the sense that by sheer weight of numbers the people make it possible for the few to develop and to apply qualities of leadership, it may be said that the people provide the opportunity of leadership.

No substitute is known as yet for population growth and density as the initial forces propelling societal development. Subject to the discovery of new forces, it must be assumed that the future development of the human society will follow the same basic pattern. New nations will take the place of existing nations. New cities, new industries, new cultures, new demands will arise. New people will play, if in different form, their traditional role as the creators of broad economic, political, social, and cultural opportunity. New leaders will create the new designs, the new dimensions, the values of a new age.

At this point, I propose to take a closer look at the basic features that set the people apart from their opposites—the persons of great aspirations, unusual abilities, and outstanding achievements—the leaders.

CHAPTER FOUR

LEADERSHIP CLASSES AS EXPLOITERS OF OPPORTUNITY

I have dealt so far with only one major aspect of the people's societal function: their contribution of massive numbers of producers and consumers and of opportunity for societal growth, as well as their loyalty, their dependence, and their struggle for physical survival.

This chapter will consider those who deal with the multitudes of producers and consumers, who exploit the opportunity for societal growth, who use the loyalty of the people and take advantage of their dependence and their struggle for physical survival. They do so by virtue of their ability to furnish ideas, know-how, design, organization, and other means needed for the attainment of their objectives. I shall call them "leaders" or, more precisely "leadership classes."

As in the case of the people, I am not dealing primarily with individual persons. Nor am I concerned with the many important types of leaders who arise in the normal process of group activity—leaders in the areas that generate social development, such as education, religion, the arts and sciences, the professions, industry, labor, agriculture, and government.

In a brief historical survey of this kind which seeks to

explain certain basic forces in societal relations, major changes and their reasons and motivations are more significant than functional patterns. I do not mean to minimize the importance of leadership on different levels, rather to seek out the kind of leadership responsible for bringing about major changes in societal living.

In this chapter, I shall deal with groups of leaders who are involved in the large dynamic activities of the human society. Therefore, by "leaders" I mean leadership classes or institutions, for example, kings, barons, slaveholders, merchant princes; and religious, military, industrial, financial, management, labor, and other hierarchies. As I inquire into the rise and fall of these leadership classes and their role in history, I want to give special attention to their relationship to the people.

NEW OPPORTUNITIES PROMOTE NEW LEADERSHIP CLASSES

By their reproductive capacity, the people make it possible to build towns and cities, to develop commerce and industry, to establish law and government, and to foster social relations and cultural attainments. Those who exploit opportunities prepared by the people benefit from the effects of population growth rather than directly from the people.

In Europe in the thirteenth century, towns and cities grew to a point where they were able to give protection and to compete successfully with the baron's castle. Trade expanded, wealth became movable, the age of commercialism dawned. The perfection of skills not only gave rise to crafts and guilds but helped to make them extremely powerful. Along with improvements in transportation and law and order, these developments played their part in altering aristocratic concepts, feudal institutions, and borders. New leadership classes arose in different countries.

In England, in 1215, the Magna Carta took the ruling power from the king and gave it to the barons and ecclesiastics in the Upper House, to the gentry and patricians in the Lower House. In Germany, later in the century, a group of vassals established themselves as Electors, with full authority to pass on the election of the German king. In France, in 1302, the barons, the clergy, and the towns were powerful enough to compel the calling of the States-General. In Spain, two decades earlier, the General Privileges of Saragossa made proud Aragon into a kind of republic ruled by the Cortes. In Italy, at about the same time, government in several cities underwent profound changes. The bishops were expelled, and government was divided between consuls elected by the aristocracy and an Upper Council to which the rising guilds appointed representatives.[1]

One important facet of the new economic opportunities in Europe was the expansion of maritime commerce and the resultant age of discovery. New leadership classes emerged.

In 1580, Sir Francis Drake returned to England with the treasures of the *Golden Hind*. This gold, which had gone through the hands of the Indians of Peru and Mexico and of the Conquistadores, made it possible for a new leadership class to establish itself and to lay the foundation for what was eventually to become the British Empire. It enabled Queen Elizabeth to pay off the national debt and, in addition, to invest the equivalent of $200,000 in an enterprise that was to become the East India Company. Compounded at 3¼ per cent from that period, this investment was estimated by John Maynard Keynes to be equal to about $20 billion in 1930, or approximately the value of prewar (1914-18) English overseas investments.[2]

In 1492, Columbus opened the way to America. The broad opportunity, considered essential to the establishment of a new leadership class, did not consist of the promise to Columbus of huge profits. Columbus' principal stipulation was that he should be invested with the full titles and privileges of admiral as well as viceroy over all the territories he discovered. He was to be given one-tenth of all gains realized either by trade or by conquest, after costs had been deducted.[3] The opportunity was reflected in the dynamic changes that had taken place over 500 years of history. The world was ready for the discovery of America in 1500, where-

57

as in 1000 AD it had been indifferent. Columbus opened a new chapter in history, whereas Leif, son of Eric the Red, merely undertook an interesting expedition.

The value of the American gold which entered sixteenth-century Europe has been estimated at $2 billion.[4] The consequences of this influx were of far-reaching importance. The gold upset the entire system of European commerce. A long and bloody battle was fought over possession of the gold. Who was to have it? The Church of Rome, which was in power? The princes, who wanted to get back into power? Or the new merchants, who were to inherit the power? The struggle led up to the Reformation of Martin Luther, the English Revolution, and the division of Europe into a continent half-Protestant, and half-Catholic. Because opportunity was ripe, Luther succeeded where John Huss had failed a hundred years before.

The modern age abounds in examples of leadership classes emerging upon new economic opportunities, as in the Arab nations, China, Indonesia, Israel, and Latin American countries. But the principle is equally true of the Norsemen who, in the ninth century AD, found opportunity in the awakening of oceanic commerce, or the Phoenicians in the fifth and the Romans in the first century BC, or the Portuguese in the fifteenth and the English in the eighteenth century AD.

Leadership classes thus exploit new economic opportunities made possible by the multiplication and concentration of the people. Far-reaching consequences of this exploitation have little effect on the people's welfare. If the concern of new leadership were primarily for the people, it would emphasize political reform and social advance. That is not the case.

PRIMARY ROLE OF
ECONOMIC OPPORTUNITY

After new leadership classes rise, they make their own opportunities. They acquire their own interests and formulate their own objectives. One of the most important objectives is the accumulation of wealth and power. The immediate motivation is often economic. In the case of financial and business leaders, the economic emphasis is self-evident. It is equally true, however, of leaders in other fields. Karl Marx was primarily concerned with economic injustice; he wanted wealth and power used in the interests of the proletariat. Jesus was strongly motivated by the economic plight of the people.

The dominant role of economic opportunity may be seen in the fact that, generally speaking, leaders who arise upon its emergence create leadership classes. Others who arise upon political rather than economic opportunity, like Alexander, Napoleon, or Hitler, may not; their passing may leave a vacuum. I have described the rise of new leadership classes upon such economic opportunities as were brought about by the voyages of Francis Drake and Columbus. One of the most recent and perhaps most convincing examples is the evolution of leadership classes in the United States, made possible primarily by the new economic opportunities of a vast undeveloped continent.

In our own age, economic opportunity has been intensified enormously and has grown to global proportions. The character of the leadership class has broadened accordingly. Industrialists and financiers share leadership with representatives of labor, the public, and other segments of society. Labor has become aware of its strength as a principal economic asset. The public has become aware of its strength as the most important source of buying power. However, the principle that the leadership class must, in order to endure, exploit new economic opportunity has remained unchanged.

This statement may be questioned. Why should the emphasis be upon economic rather than political or social factors? Obviously, no leadership class can hope to survive unless it combines economic success with an effective social pattern and a political credo of some significance. It is true that air-conditioning, color television, and frozen foods, as much as full employment, high wages, pension plans, and the five-day week were made possible by a new leadership class, with its inventive genius and managerial ability. However, its success is predicated on the democratic way of life and on the principles of equal opportunity and competitive enterprise, all of which are political concepts and social patterns. In the Soviet Union, the emphasis on the attainment of economic goals through such means as the Five-Year Plans and the concentration upon heavy industry was made possible by a carefully worked-out and strictly controlled political doctrine and social system. The political and social factors match, if they do not indeed surpass, the economic factor in importance.

Different economic opportunities in different countries have created different leadership classes and different interpretations of how best to exploit these opportunities. The communist dogma of the Soviet Union, the socialist dogma of New Zealand, and the democratic dogma of the United States represent different interpretations of the way each leadership class thinks it best to combine economic opportunity, social goals, and political power.

Besides, why single out economic opportunity as created by the people? Do not the people also create political and social opportunity by supporting and electing candidates, by making possible political parties and government, by consuming goods and using services, and by making possible a high level of employment as well as a high standard of living?

The answer is that leadership classes are apt to collapse when economic opportunities change on the grand scale. The founders of the American republic were replaced by traders and early manufacturers, who were replaced by railroad builders and explorers of the West, who were replaced by public utilities magnates and financiers, who were replaced by corporate management, and so on and on. Leadership classes are less likely to collapse when political opportunities change—unless economic factors are responsible. In fact, such opportunities (if on a major scale) are not only tied up with but caused by economic changes. For example, changes in the political opportunities of the Civil War period were caused by the ascendancy of the industrial North over the agricultural South; and desegregation in our own age was caused by new economic opportunities for the black population. Changes in purely political opportunities seem to occur mostly on the local or regional level as fluctuations in political issues and local problems. They rarely involve the opportunities and aspirations of leadership classes.

From the viewpoint of the leadership class, the attainment of economic goals is probably more important in the long run than the attainment of either social or political goals. Economic control means control of economic assets, which is the principal aim of most leadership classes, past and present. Priests and kings controlled the treasury; tribal chiefs and patriarchs controlled slaves and herds; merchant princes controlled credits; barons controlled castles; feudal lords controlled the land and the peasants. By contrast, political control covers mostly votes, and those only for a limited time. More often than not, the voters are influenced, if not controlled, by those who control economic assets, as the Hitler regime was controlled by the Junkers and their allies.

Economic opportunities, and the wealth and power that accompany their exploitation, are more enduring than political opportunities and the power derived from them. Leaders arising upon the latter are often motivated by short-range personal aspirations, as was the case with Napoleon. Political leaders are mostly opportunists. This is not true to the same degree of leaders arising upon economic opportunity. Caesar, Drake, Columbus, Clyde, the Astors, and the Vanderbilts may have been opportunists, but their enterprise was either built upon new economic opportunity or happened to coincide with it. Moreover, they were instrumental in building, developing, and controlling large economic assets, and their enterprise led to the evolution of leadership classes. These facts give their work a more enduring importance. Economic opportunities are the result of great changes taking place in the destinies of human societies, such as the building of the Roman Empire (Caesar), the decline of the Roman Empire (Jesus), the building of the British Empire (Clyde), or the decline of the British Empire (Gandhi). Compared with these basic, enduring changes, political opportunities, such as the Nazis exploited, have more of a transient significance.

Another reason for the importance of economic opportunity is that economics, which involves physical survival, is more basic to the interests of the people than politics or even social programs. Since major leadership requires a major

61

following, economics must be a principal concern of the leadership class.

Of the three opportunities, only the economic one is highly and originally dynamic; political and social opportunities are more likely to be the results of dynamic economic opportunity. They are subject to change as soon as new economic opportunity brings forth a new leadership class, which eventually will change both the political power structure and the social pattern. This distinction between the primary character of new economic opportunities and the secondary character of political and social factors indicates that leadership classes do not fail so much because of political or social factors as because of changing economic opportunities.

DIFFERENT TYPES OF LEADERSHIP CLASSES

As economic opportunities change, so do the character and creative ability of leadership classes. Different economic opportunities produce different types of leadership classes.

At this point in American history, the new leadership class can no longer rise on the strength of all-round economic control. Unlike its predecessors, the new American leadership class can no longer dominate the entire economic scene. The scene has grown too complex. The new class can control only that part of the economic whole which, in its judgment, promises maximum wealth and power. Leadership thus becomes expert in the development of new industries, the design of new corporate systems, the organization of new groups, the application of new methods, or the formulation of new contracts and treaties. For full control, the leadership class also would have to be expert in labor matters, public relations, taxation, psychology, statesmanship, and other fields. The coming age will speak increasingly of labor leadership, management leadership, scientific leadership, technological leadership, sociological leadership, and so on. This division of hierarchies is likely to accentuate the conflict between the various interests in pursuit of wealth and power.

In China, the Soviet Union, and the United States, the type of emerging leadership classes is different because the nature of economic opportunity is different. In the creative sense, the quality of leadership should be of the highest order in the rapidly developing countries like China. Her leadership class must possess a highly constructive imagination, for it must create the pattern of the economic evolution. Possessing neither the mastery of the industrial equipment, the advantages of world finance, or a sophisticated economic organization—all of which are required for the creation of massive wealth—the leadership class of the new China must furnish ideas along with ideals, inspiration along with design.

What will the Chinese leadership class choose as the best form of the national evolution: the communist society, the cooperative, the republic, the commonwealth, the socialist pattern, the continental structure, or the empire model? Will it build upon the tradition of the yellow race or experiment with the fruits of white civilization? Will it create wealth merely by imitation of the occidental example or can it pull out of the millennia of its own history a brand-new (to whites) formula? The young leadership class of the new China is holding in its hands a mass of clay. Clear and far vision, combined with true creative ability, will mold it into meaningful shape and productive substance.

In the Soviet Union, well along on the road to great wealth, the new leadership class has shifted from the level of vivid imagination and solid creativeness, as existed in the Lenin-Tolstoy era, to the level that stresses the value of scientific formulas. Instead of forceful and original interpretation, further progress will require careful measurement and judgment. The industrial equipment is available, the financial means are provided, the economic (as well as political and social) organization developed to a substantial degree. No great amount of fresh originality and creative vision seems to be needed for the Soviet Union's further economic development. Perhaps the need does not go beyond the application of known and proven means to new fields.

The task of the new leadership class is to intensify, to accelerate, and to enlarge economic development. Once the key to the exploitation of natural wealth has been found, the creation of new wealth will develop practically by its own momentum. The process taking place in the Soviet Union today was completed in the United States three or four generations ago. Then new wealth rolled in, as it were, under its own power from the vast forests, the rich mines, the long waterways, and the new railroads and utilities. The only prerequisite was an economic organization that needed ore, lumber, and transportation facilities to satisfy the growing needs of the land and its people.

The leadership class in a highly developed country such as the United States must master technical know-how, be it in engineering, law, management, labor, finance, or other fields where the attainment of greater wealth and greater power is the primary goal. With this in mind, it can hardly be said that the United States has such a profound problem of choice as modern China has. Hence, it has limited opportunity for truly creative leadership in the economic domain. Would not future expansion mean the extension of the sphere of influence from continental to global dimensions? Would not greater wealth mean the conversion from a partly into a fully industrialized economy? Is it not true that only industry can create new wealth upon a large scale? Therefore, if the United States is to attain still greater wealth, must it not intensify the industrial development, building gigantic power dams and constructing huge plants across the belt and down the spine of the nation? Does it mean obtaining larger quantities of foodstuffs and raw materials from neighboring or overseas countries? Does it mean keeping armed to the teeth so as to maintain (or to gain) control of marketing and supply areas, including global lines of communication?

Faced with this panoramic vista, the new type of leadership in the United States must prove its mastery not of creation but of aggrandizement. New wealth will be produced by its ability to build a plant twice as fast, a dam twice as high, a road half as cheap as was possible before. The new leadership must have the ingenuity to expand the existing economic organization enormously. But that is a different challenge than the creation of a radically new economic pattern.

In these different ways, a highly developed nation like the United States produces the utilitarian type of leadership marked by technical and managerial skill and know-how, while a young nation like modern China produces creative leadership. One type owes its rise to war, the other emerges in peace. The type of leadership that prepares economic opportunity is distinguished by vision, faith, courage. The founders of the American republic and some of their successors are a good example. The type that harvests the crop and cashes in on opportunity is typified more often by administrative and managerial ability; often it has an unemotional attitude toward the people since its campaign is primarily one of utilization.

There are leadership classes of all types because there are economic opportunities of all kinds: the nation at birth and the nation in decay; the nation in adolescence and the nation in maturity; the opportunity of peace and that of war; there is the dream of a better future for mankind, and there is the inexorable drive for power. None of these types of leadership classes is either all good or all bad; each is the result of conditions that, through the instrument of the people, bring about the opportunities on which leadership thrives.

65

TRANSITORY NATURE OF LEADERSHIP CLASSES

The primary role of new economic opportunity is reflected in the transitory nature of leadership classes. Often, leaders have sought to outlast economic opportunity by perpetuating their individual dominance; they have rarely succeeded. The leaders who are in power during one period of economic opportunity rarely predominate in the next. The leaders who win a war are not generally the ones who exploit the opportunities of victory. New opportunity does not compromise with old leaders.

Alexander of Macedonia might have been surprised could he have seen the crop of leaders who tried to exploit the opportunities he had helped create. The abuses committed by his generals, the gradual collapse of Hellenism, and the influx of barbarian power were hardly what Alexander and the leaders of his day must have envisioned for the glory of Greater Hellas.

The leaders who helped Julius Caesar to power were not the ones who derived the greatest benefit from his accomplishments. It is probably incorrect to call Caesar the founder of the Roman monarchy; the trend toward a monarchical form of government had begun long before Caesar's time. But it may be accurate to state that he was instrumental in creating the opportunity upon which the leadership class of Imperial Rome arose. The difference is that Caesar served as the instrument rather than the deliberate designer of the greatness of Rome.

Francisco Pizarro's small band of armored knights conquered the Incas and were rewarded with huge chunks of land, but they exploited none of it because opportunity was not ripe. The soil of Peru lay waste until three centuries later when the merchants and engineers of Europe and other lands came with their farming, mining, and railroad equipment to make something of the opportunity Pizarro's conquest had initiated.

Turning to England's wars in India: many nabobs returned home with large fortunes, determined to win social position and political power. Some gained seats in the House of Commons. These men who exploited the opportunity opened up by the Indian campaigns were not the original settlers, nor the soldiers, nor their commanders.[5]

The leaders themselves are usually the last to see the limitations of their opportunity or the transitory nature of their accomplishments. Napoleon expected his leadership class to shape the future of Europe. Instead, his fall helped bring about the resurrection of a strong central Europe and the gradual disappearance of French predominance on the continent. Perhaps no one did so much to dig the grave of France as the leading continental power as the man who wanted to be the godfather of her glorious future.

The leaders in the thirteen colonies at the end of the Revolutionary War were not those who reaped the harvest of new economic opportunity. While Washington, Franklin,

Adams, and others acquired substantial property, the early representatives of the rising leadership class were busy buying furs at six cents in the Northwest and selling them in China for a hundred dollars a piece.⁶ They were buying clocks and kitchenware cheap in Connecticut and selling them high in Charleston. They were importing tin plates, copper sheets, and rolls of wire from Liverpool to start the domestic metal industry. They were building the first machines, the first steamboats and locomotives, and running the first trains. They were the real exploiters of the economic opportunities marking the period that began roughly with the death of Washington and ended with the death of Lincoln.

The next era, roughly from the Reconstruction Period to the end of the century, saw the rise of a different leadership class. It started new industries (mining, lumber, and those resulting from the internal-combustion engine and the electric dynamo) and new patterns of living. It pushed the westward expansion until there was no frontier left. It made experimentation in the tool shed and research in the laboratory sources of great achievement. Notwithstanding the amazing achievements of this leadership class, in the light of subsequent developments the era may almost be called one of preparation. Nor were many of the pioneers overly successful in the material sense.

The real exploiters of new economic opportunities flourished in the first quarter of the twentieth century: Ford, General Motors, U.S. Steel, J. P. Morgan, Standard Oil, General Electric, along with the American Federation of Labor, and many others. Both these leadership classes contributed to the creation of new wealth, with the difference that the former, operating in the second half of the nineteenth century, needed the wealth; while the latter, operating in the first half of the twentieth century, made most of it. At first, the inventors (McCormick, Westinghouse, Edison) stimulated the managers, investors, and entrepreneurs. Later, the managers and entrepreneurs stimulated inventors, technicians, and scientists to produce the means for the creation of still greater wealth.

Whatever the changes in new economic opportunities, however, the attainment of wealth and (through wealth) of power, remains the unchanging objective of leadership classes.

LACK OF OPPORTUNITY DESTROYS LEADERSHIP CLASSES

The importance of economic opportunity is perhaps shown most clearly, if negatively, in the failure of leadership classes. Long before their eventual collapse, many signs indicate their inability to meet the challenge of newly arising opportunity. Sometimes, the signs are misleading; the display of wealth at the top may hide the widening crack at the bottom. The inability of a leadership class to meet new conditions and problems expresses itself in such manifestations as high taxes, expanded government controls, inflation, unemployment, and general stagnation.

Four hundred years before its collapse, the Roman Empire showed signs of internal stress. Extended lines of communication were sagging under the weight of military and commercial traffic; an inadequate monetary system weakened under the weight of rising prices; a sterile economy was hardly helped by growing corruption, wasteful spending, and luxurious living by a small minority. Never corrected, these and related defects contributed heavily to the breakdown of the empire.[7] On the other hand, the situation created new opportunity for the slaves skilled in arts and crafts. Fighting tradition and the ancient exclusiveness of Roman society, the slaves rose from menial service to professional recognition. Ignored before, they were now held in considerable esteem, though they could not save the empire.

In its dying days, ancient Egypt resembled an automaton rather than an empire. Frozen by the dictates of the priestly hierarchy, arts and sciences stood still. The human figure must be drawn in ever the same manner, with the same proportions, the same contours, and the same colors. Sons must take up the professions of the fathers and must marry within their own classes. The Egyptian robot had priests for the head, soldiers for arms, workers for feet. Then came the collapse.[8]

The opportunities of clearing and cultivating the lower valley and delta of the Nile, of unifying the country, of developing forms of writing, of carrying out great engineering projects, of making important contributions in the arts and sciences—opportunities that had been exploited to a remarkable degree by the leadership classes of the Old Kingdom—had disappeared. New conditions had arisen. Apart from fighting the invaders (the Hyksos, the Assyrians, the sea-raiders), the leadership classes during the two thousand years after the Old Kingdom were incapable of meeting the new conditions, let alone of creating new opportunities.

The same lack of initiative and ability marked the later kings of the Persian Empire who spent their time in leisure and luxury. Leaving the affairs of government to hirelings, they invited corruption and mismanagement. The end was not far off.[9]

Another example of the inadequacy that marks the decline and eventual death of leadership classes is Louis XVI who went hunting on Bastille Day; he could think of nothing more memorable to record in his diary than the word "Nothing." Or Tsar Nicholas who, in a similar crisis, wrote in his diary "walked long and killed two crows; had tea by daylight. . . ."[10]

69

Whether Louis XV, XVI, or the Stuarts, whether George III or Tsar Nicholas, the common feature preceding the collapse of the leadership class was a weak and incompetent government. While the leaders were unwilling to give up their claim to the new opportunities, they knew no better than to trust the old methods. High taxes, dispossessions, inflation, and expanded government authority are hardly the answer to new opportunities. The burghers faced the feudal lords; the commoners, Charles I; the American colonists, George III; the French Third Estate, Louis XVI and the First and Second Estates. In each case, the ruling class was unable to cope with the new conditions, the new demands, the new opportunities.[11]

Stagnation arises when new opportunity is ignored by the existing system. The economic revolution of the thirteenth century

> eventually destroyed a feudalism that had completed the function of agricultural protection and organization, and had become an obstacle to the expansion of enterprise. It transformed the immobile wealth of feudalism into the fluent resources of a worldwide economy. It provided the machinery for a progressive development of business and industry. [12]

Again, as in the case of the slaves in ancient Rome, the situation created new opportunity for a class that had been until then without prestige in the social hierarchy. The new commercialism made the lack of adequate banking and credit facilities acutely felt. The Jewish moneylenders were the only ones able to meet the situation. While the leaders of society looked down upon these technicians of wealth, they tolerated their assistance. [13]

In ancient times, it took centuries to develop new economic opportunity. By contrast, the modern dynamic economy produces one or more new major opportunities every generation. The leaders who were instrumental in the enactment of the Constitution were slow in promoting the territorial aggrandizement of the new republic; they were replaced by Jefferson's Agrarian Party. During the sixty years from Jefferson's to Lincoln's inauguration, all but two of the presidents were affiliated with that party. When the agrarian leaders failed to exploit the opportunities of overseas commerce, they quickly faded from the scene. [14]

The characteristic stagnation of the leadership class prior to its collapse may be seen in the South before the Civil War. It hardly required special foresight to realize the advantages of the machine. But pride and class consciousness, inherited wealth, and rewarding monopoly prevented the southern aristocracy from feeling the desire, let alone the need, to abandon the slave system. The new economic opportunity, plainly written across the face of the continent, meant little to the southern leadership class. It did not respond to the challenge of a new age.

In the twentieth century, stagnation again forecasts new

70

economic opportunities and the coming of a new leadership class. In his book *The Managerial Revolution*, James Burnham notes some of the manifestations of the stagnation process. Since the end of the First World War, there has been only one change in the listing of the first sixty families in the United States. The inability of a ruling class to assimilate new blood is a symptom of its decadence and approaching decline.[15] The big capitalists, he continues, who legally are the principal owners of the instruments of production, have gradually separated themselves from this final source and base of social dominance. First, they withdrew from production to finance; then, they retired from active and direct participation in the economic process, preferring to spend their time in social diversions. Leaving the management of their financial interests to others, eventually they lost control.

> The propertied class is opposed to change because its entire economic position rests upon inheritance and vested rights. Since it takes its title from the past, it cannot let the past be discredited. Since most reforms are detrimental to property, the propertied have an horror of all radical ideas.[16]

Writing between the two world wars, thinkers like James Burnham and Sidney Reeve have argued that capitalism is dying out and have cited some of the problems that must be solved if new opportunities are to be exploited. Among the problems are: the rise of private and public debt to unmanageable proportions; the cessation of free monetary exchange caused by gold hoarding and barter agreements; a twenty-year agricultural depression; lack of investment opportunity; the retarded economic development of countries in Asia, Africa, Latin America, the Mediterranean Basin, and other areas; and the prevalence of an important bourgeois ideology.

As this is written three decades later, a few problems may be added: high and rising taxes; growing inflation; increasing central authority; weakening personal responsibility; the oversized corporation; widespread graft and corruption. These and related problems may indicate the widening crack at the bottom of the national economy. While the problems may not be solved, it does not mean that the growth of the American nation may not continue, and the wealth of the economy may not increase for a long while yet—as it did in the case of ancient Rome.

The time schedule in the decline of leadership classes varies. In countries where new economic opportunity is slow to develop, as in Latin America, the change in leadership classes may be determined by popular unrest, rebellion, and violence rather than by the rise of new economic opportunity, although the two may hang together. The fall of the Peron regime in Argentina is a case in point. In countries like the United States where a dynamic economy makes for the rapid development of new economic opportunity, the turnover in leadership classes is equally rapid. The milestones marking periods of stagnation, new economic opportunities, and the rise of new leadership classes are clearly seen in American history:

Jackson—beginning of the factory era;
Lincoln—beginning of northern industrialism;
Cleveland—beginning of the power era;
Theodore Roosevelt—beginning of the corporate era;
Franklin Roosevelt—beginning of the atomic (?) era.

Where new opportunities have been tied to a great personality, the elimination of the leadership class is ruthless and tragic. The pages of history are filled with its victims. Upon the death of Charlemagne, the empire of the Franks fell into decay. Invaders, says T. B. Macaulay, came "as if by concert" from the far corners of the earth: pirates of the northern sea, Magyars, Saracens.[17]

Upon the death of the great Aurangzeb, India was attacked from all sides. The Persians crossed the Indus and took the treasures of Delhi. The Afghans followed. The Sikhs ruled on the Indus, the Jats among the Jumna. The terrible Mahrattas descended from the mountains and subdued most of India.[18]

For the dynamic development of society, the death of an old leadership class is as important as the birth of new opportunity. Speaking of the collapse of the Frank empire, Macaulay says:

> the corruption of death fermented into new forms of life. Here, in the most barren and dreary tract of European history, all feudal privileges, all modern nobility take their source. [19]

CHAPTER
FIVE

FORMS
AND
PHASES
OF
OPPORTUNITY

Perhaps no medium has created so much new economic as well as social and political oportunity in such abundance, with such force, and with such regularity, as the medium of war.

WAR AND ECONOMIC OPPORTUNITY

"War is the father of all things," said the Ionian philosopher Heraclitus. This may be overstating the case, but history leaves little doubt that by its destruction of old and its introduction of new forms (nations and civilizations, ideas and symbols, inventions and skills, institutions and cultures), war has been a most powerful instrument of new opportunity. War is the enemy of normalcy. So is the rising leader who finds his opportunity in the things that are alien and often seemingly contrary to the ruling interests. War creates the emergency which creates the need and the market for new aspirations, ideas, and energies.

The first "American" leadership emerged from the struggles of the first Indian wars. The constant threats of arrow, torch, and tomahawk made the settlers quickly aware of the men among them who had courage, resourcefulness, and wisdom. These men were not only able to lead but willing to sacrifice personal interests to the collective need. They had the strength and the authority to enforce their commands, the prudence to restrain their people, and the tenacity to hold on in the face of slim odds. New leadership emerges where the challenge of danger or opportunity is met by these and related qualities. Rarely are these qualities tested more thoroughly than in war.

In the past, war has often been the key to a nation's greatness. Napoleon, like many other leaders, knew that. What he learned too late, and what most leaders do not seem to want to learn, was that no single regime or leadership class can underwrite enduring national greatness. Its establishment usually takes several wars, each of which creates new opportunity, each of which challenges a new leadership class.

The impact of war upon new economic opportunity has become more far-reaching as war has raised its sights, broadened its scope, and intensified its effort. In our own time, the need for a leadership class capable of realizing the vast opportunities created by the Second World War, has become more difficult to meet than ever before. Tomorrow's opportunities no longer involve one nation or group of nations. They involve Mankind.

War marks the progress of every expanding state or nation. The leaders of ancient Rome found frequent opportunity in war. Rome carried on warfare with the tribes of Italy for 65 years, with Gaul for 20 years, Carthage for 45 years. These included only major campaigns; many others were of less imposing size and duration. In ancient Greece, warfare previous to the rule of Philip and Alexander consumed 50 years. Subsequent wars within or about Alexander's empire consumed another 85 years. Again, these were only the more important military campaigns. '

The Franks were highly successful in early medieval Europe. Probably none among the Frank leaders fought more wars than Charlemagne who, with his sons and generals, undertook no fewer than 54 campaigns; of these, eighteen were against the Saxons, seven against the Saracens in Spain, five against the Lombards, five against the Arabs in Italy. Only one year in his long reign, 781, was without war. [2]

Wars then being hardly more than summer campaigns, the opportunity created by each war was limited in scope. But even though the campaigns were on a comparatively small scale, the Franks exploited each opportunity so effectively that they were able to expand their insignificant tribe to a great empire.

The initial development of the American colonies was due to the enterprise of Spanish, Dutch, French, and English leaders. After the first gains had been consolidated, a new leadership class arose. Blocked by the English hierarchy, the challenge of new economic opportunity used the instrument of war (the Revolutionary War) to defeat it. After the war had been won, an agricultural leadership class arose to exploit and to consolidate the internal gains. When the industrial ascendancy of the North was opposed by the established agricultural hierarchy of the South, the Civil War stripped the old leadership of its economic dominance, thus clearing the way for the industrial class.

New economic opportunity was exploited to the point of abuse, as shown in the speculative orgy of railroad, mining, and public utility enterprise. The Spanish-American War heralded the arrival of a new leadership class, including financiers, imperialists, and world merchants. By 1914, the gains derived from this expansion had been digested. Another leadership class was to be promoted by the opportunities gained with victory in the First World War. Possibly due to a basic transformation of the American society, industrial, financial, and other interests failed to rise to the traditional challenge. They did not produce a new leadership class. Instead, a new class arose in the hierarchy of labor and government.

Their primary interest is not the pursuit of wealth but the pursuit of power. If appealed to for peace, the leaders would probably answer, and rightly so, that they do not want war. They want to perpetuate and, if possible, strengthen their power and influence.

The dynamics of human aspirations, as seen in the history of nations, cause opportunity to fluctuate constantly between peace and war; history has confirmed it through the centuries. Opportunity remains the fixed pole in the flight of human ideas.

WAR IN CONTEMPORARY HISTORY

A primary question in the discussion of the role of war in contemporary history concerns the effect of atomic warfare. A strong body of world opinion argues that atomic warfare can be safely discounted because its consequences are too horrible to contemplate. Two counterarguments are made: first, past history has abundant evidence that anticipated horrors have never yet prevented a major war; and second, the invention of a weapon of attack has invariably been followed in due time by the invention of a defensive device which will weaken if not neutralize the weapon of attack. Both counterarguments are historically true. I believe that the basic causes of war are so deeply rooted not only in the aspirations of nations but in the very system of human society that only a radical change of the societal system, such as is discussed and analyzed in this volume, is likely to bring about a decided change in the traditional role of war. Until then, I believe that war must be reckoned with as a key factor, although perhaps in forms, methods, and degrees of intensity quite different from those of the past.

How, then, does the traditional role of war fit into contemporary history? Has the time come for a new leadership class? If it has arrived, how does it interpret (and propose to exploit) the new opportunities that have been beckoning since victory in the Second World War? What might be the meaning (historically speaking) of recent and future wars, hot or cold?

Russia's revolution of 1917 brought victory for communism, defeat for tsarism. The latter proved incapable of meeting economic needs simmering beneath the ashes of a decrepit leadership class, while communism proved capable of meeting the most pressing needs through organized action and tangible achievement. It took three wars (the Crimean, the Russo-Japanese, the First World War) to bring the issue to a head. It took the Second World War to make it clear that the leadership class of the communist ideology had served its purpose and would be replaced by a class representing a different ideology, even though the same in name.

From the Crimean to Hitler's war, the basic issue did not lie between Tsarists and Bolsheviks; East and West; Russia on the one side, England, France, Germany on the other. The principal issue lay between the inability of the old leadership class to cope with economic needs, and the ability of the rising leadership class to meet them. It is from the first of these revolutionary efforts led by Ivan Turgenev and Nikolai Chernyshevsky about a hundred years before the 1917 revolution and continued by Aleksandr Herzen and Mikhail Bakunin that the post-tsarist leadership class takes its origin. The social problem of industrialism, along with its promise of new economic opportunity, began to make itself felt in the 1860's. The last and most powerful representative of that leadership class was Joseph Stalin.

Following the Second World War the new leadership class took the industrial predominance initiated by the Lenin-Stalin hierarchy as its leitmotif. According to the historical pattern the new class should now prepare for the successful prosecution of the next war, thereby digging its own grave and rocking the cradle of the succeeding leadership class. Whether it will follow the historical pattern remains to be seen.

In the dynamic current of human affairs, communism is little more than a stage in a historical cycle. As a political dogma, it is likely to be short-lived. Actually, it is a powerful expression of the evolutionary force of economic and social-political opportunity. As opportunity broadens and new leadership classes arise, communism may gradually fade as an instrument of domestic policy although it may continue to serve effectively as an instrument of foreign policy. Nowhere is this more true than in China.

China's recent history points to the rebirth of a great nation. There are new concepts of land utilization and vast new visions of wealth creation. There are new concepts of the application of power—military, economic, political, and social. Most important, there are the people, newly inspired and deeply dedicated. Of course, there are the wars creating new opportunities: the Boxer Rebellion, the First Japanese War, and the climactic struggle with the Japanese Empire. The future greatness of modern China indicates the agony of her future wars.

No age emerging from a long period of darkness, confusion, and discord can be created by the people alone. It is the task of the rising leadership class to shape the new age. Where a middle class exists, its experience helps bring about orderly progress through organization, industry, and economy. In early America, the European experience of middle-class people proved of value to the rising leadership class. The people produced lumber, furs, tobacco, and many other products which helped new classes to acquire wealth and power. But where, as in China, the masses have been living for centuries in the dull, uninspiring atmosphere of unquestioned obedience, where poverty has been the accepted standard, and the search for food the daily need, the appeal to enlightened self-interest is a new and daring experiment.

Yet communism has proved the most effective means of rallying the dull, the unenlightened, the poor, and the helpless to an extraordinary economic effort without which the new opportunity could not have been realized so quickly. Leaving aside the means employed, the ultimate result does not differ from the goal of democratic, autocratic, or other forms of government: furtherance of the national aspiration. Ideological principles are for the cause of mankind but practical policies are in the interest of the nation.

Thus, practical communism may be judged essentially a form of nationalism and, if extended, of imperialism. As the voice of organized poverty, it is the chief protagonist of new economic opportunity. A kind of communism existed among some of the early American settlers. But no sooner had scarcity given way to a degree of economic security, no sooner had material opportunity shown its great promise than communism disappeared from the American scene. Gradually, the Soviet Union is building its material prosperity, its consumer production, and its other forms of economic security. As it loses its natural breeding grounds, communism nears the end of its usefulness. It will find more fertile grounds elsewhere. The experience is likely to be repeated in areas of widespread poverty in Asia, Africa, and Latin America.

While communism has proved to be the instrument through which the poor may effectively assert their rights, war has proved to be the instrument through which the nation effectively asserts its interests and aspirations. Poverty is no excuse for exemption from serving the national interest.

FOUR PHASES OF OPPORTUNITY

In the contemporary world, four phases of opportunity for the creation of new leadership classes may be distinguished:

The first phase is found in a country like Great Britain where dynamic opportunity on the grand scale is past history. After much creation and exploitation of economic opportunity, the contemporary leadership class can no longer respond dynamically to new opportunity. Its actions therefore take the form of government control, collective action, and socialization of coal mines, public utilities, and other industries. No future war is likely to produce opportunity for new leadership classes to create new wealth on a large scale. If successful, wars will do no more than to slow down the process of disintegration. No creative leadership can blossom in an atmosphere where protection is perhaps the only promise. New dynamic opportunity shifts increasingly from the motherland to the former empire members.

The second phase of opportunity is found in the history of the United States. Although perhaps not by design, wars have been and are being fought for growth and expansion and for the creation of new opportunity and new leadership classes. The colonial wars were fought for the acquisition of land; the War of Independence, for the creation of a new nation; the

Civil War, for industrial growth; the Spanish War, for overseas expansion, if on a small scale; the First World War, for the opportunity of gaining economic independence from European ties and, at the same time, international influence; the Second World War, for the opportunity to advance from a continental power into a leading world power.

Each war produced new economic opportunities and a new leadership class: the leaders in Virginia and New England; those around Jefferson and Hamilton; the new manufacturers, the merchants and clipper captains; the speculators and railroad builders; the miners and inventors; the international bankers; the corporation organizers; the managers. None gave thanks to the wars that gave them their opportunity. Perhaps it is correct to say that none had wanted war. Yet each leadership class in its turn grasped the opportunity as soon as it appeared. It can hardly be doubted that similar principles will apply in the future. For the United States, it would appear that the greatest opportunity is still ahead because the greatest economic expansion may yet be ahead—and perhaps the greatest war.

The third phase of opportunity is found in the Soviet Union. Whereas in the United States the organized exploitation of economic opportunity has been going on since the last third of the nineteenth century, in the Soviet Union it began at the end of the Second World War and has not yet been completed. Opportunity is just appearing in all its enormity. Stalin is but the progenitor of all subsequent leadership classes; Lenin is but a legend. The Second World War is but the first of the wars fought for economic and political expansion. The leadership class that won it was not the one to exploit the opportunities created by its victory; nor will the latter be the one to open the door to the greater wealth and power now in sight.

The fourth phase of opportunity is as yet in the future of modern China. The outline (though dim) is impressive in its suggested contours. The wars (mostly cold) that are being fought are perhaps expressions of internal strife in the communist world rather than designs of expansion. The new leadership class which may exploit future opportunities is still in the cradle. The wars that may confirm China as a great world power of far-reaching influence may yet be fought. The opportunities may yet crystallize into forms bearing a precise relationship to the rest of the world.

As of the late sixties and early seventies, the new dynamic and highly creative economic opportunity appears embryonic in China, as it appears moribund in Great Britain, mature in the United States, and adolescent in the Soviet Union.

THE PEOPLE'S WELFARE IS NOT THE PRIME INTEREST OF LEADERSHIP CLASSES

Through the centuries, all major leadership was made possible by the conditions created, if unwittingly, by the people —either by their high birth rate or migration or both. To state the historical experience another way: without the people settling the land and congregating in towns and cities, the development of leadership classes would not have been possible. Did the development benefit the people? Was their welfare a major or perhaps even the primary consideration?

Religious leadership classes, as initiated by Confucius, Buddha, Moses, Jesus, and Mohammed, have done much for the welfare of the people, not only in the spiritual but also in the material sense. However, notwithstanding their far-reaching charitable activities, the great religions have not eliminated poverty, insecurity, dependence, or the struggle for bare survival on the part of most of the world's population. Has any world religion ever been so organized as to make the welfare of the people its primary objective? Or is (and must be) the permanent objective of any religion to protect, to preserve, and, if possible, to strengthen its identity and autonomy? For that matter, can any major religious organization be reoriented and restructured so as to make the welfare of the people its unquestioned primary objective?

Political leadership classes, as initiated by Lincoln, Disraeli, Bismarck, Lenin, and many others, have furthered the welfare of the people. However, their primary objective was to advance the interests of nation or empire, to which the welfare of the people was subordinate. It would appear from the historical record that no national government has made, is making, or perhaps can make the welfare of the people its long-term primary objective.

Economic leadership classes, as initiated by German industrialists, English financiers, and American Vanderbilts, Fords and Rockefellers, contributed much to the welfare of the people. While most of the people of the world did not gain economic security, in some parts they did score inprovements in standards of living, comfort, sanitation, hygiene, and other conditions. Again, the primary objective of these groups was the attainment of financial success and, with it, influence and power rather than the welfare of the people, which was secondary.

Labor leadership classes, as initiated by Marx, Engels, Kautsky, etc., have made perhaps the greatest contribution of all these classes to the material welfare of the people during a comparatively short period of time. However, this originally primary concern gave way to a growing interest on the part of the labor hierarchy in the attainment of ever greater power and influence. The welfare of the people became a secondary objective.

Notwithstanding the occasional beneficial effects upon various groups of people, leadership classes have not changed the basic economic and political status of the people in most parts of the world, have not done away with principles as well as practices of exploitation and even servitude, and have not narrowed the gap between the people and leadership classes. Often, they have widened it.

A case in point is the experience in the United States. The founding fathers were political statesmen and spiritual leaders as well as economic masters. Fifty and a hundred years later, leadership had been transferred to inventors, speculators, financiers, and managers. But the Morgans, Harrimans, Vanderbilts, and Edisons were far from statesmanship, farther yet from spiritual leadership.

The leadership classes of today and tomorrow are likely to move still farther away from the lives, interests, and aspirations of the common people. Increasingly, they will deal in slogans that demand the masses to listen but not the individual to speak. The world will applaud their wealth-making and power-building performance but may wonder why the gap keeps widening between the leadership classes and the people.

IDENTITY OF LEADERSHIP

The orientation of a leader's aspirations is identified not so much by his attitudes to his followers as by his relationship with his opposite players. The labor leader who consistently refuses to make new demands upon employers will soon be replaced as a labor leader. The religious leader who does not clearly distinguish his church's interpretation of man's relation to God from the interpretation of other churches will soon find himself without understanding and without members. The government leader who does not insist upon the interests of his nation as distinct from (and, if necessary, opposed to) the interests of other nations will betray the office entrusted to him.

In order to survive, leaders must maintain their identity by the principle of distinction. In order to succeed, they must accentuate the principle. There is no surer way to fail than to ignore it.

Before Alexander the Great reached the pinnacle of success, he made his advance not by reconciling but by sharpening the distinctions separating Macedonia from the Greek city states, the Persian and other civilizations. Luther succeeded not by reconciling but by sharpening the dogmas differing from those of the Roman Church. England owed its enormous success during the eighteenth and nineteenth centuries to a form of government, commercial policies, and a military and naval system unique to the English nation and, later, to the British Empire. Its identity was kept in sharp and precise distinction to the governments, policies, and military systems of other national organizations.

Conversely, the greater the willingness to compromise, the greater the threat to the survival of leadership or even of the nation. Akhenaten brought ancient Egypt nearly to ruin by his enlightened, unselfish, and conciliatory attitude. Baldwin and Chamberlain endangered the security and even the survival of the British Empire by their conciliatory attitude toward Hirohito, Mussolini, and Hitler. We have already noted the exceptional case of King Asoka of India who abolished warfare and devoted his reign to disseminating the teachings of Buddha.

The need for leaders to adhere to and if possible to strengthen the identity of their group as it differs from the identities of other groups makes it virtually impossible for them to help all the people. Generally, leaders are not free to choose their own course. The head of a government may be an ardent believer in peace, yet he must lead his nation into war if the interests of the nation dictate such a course.

The people around the world are separated not primarily by their own feelings and opinions but by the conflicting interests of their leaders. If the American people distrust the Russian people, if the African people loathe the British people, if the Arab people hate the Israeli people, it is not because some are better off than others. It is because the people are carriers of a tradition, heirs to a prejudice, subjects of a nation or race, serving the interests and policies determined by their leaders. It is in this division of allegiance that loyalty and cooperation on the one side and animosity and hatred on the other are rooted and flourish.

While leaders will generally adhere to the identity of the group they serve, creative leadership will find ways to assert its genius and impose its ideas upon the collective. Creative leadership is identified by its ability to conceive new ideas and to bring them to fruition. To be meaningful, new ideas must differ from existing ideas. To be effective, they must replace existing ideas. To the extent that the new ideas affect the institutions of the human society, dynamic leadership is responsible for the long-term development of societal institutions.

Religion has been an institution of human society for thousands of years. New ideas such as monotheism replaced old ideas such as paganism. Leadership classes developed by the Hebrew tribes were responsible for the elaboration of these ideas. Rather than accept the institutions as they found them, leaders set about to refine institutional concepts and thus to improve the institutions themselves. In this process, the leaders played a decisive part.

Unless leaders have the ability to change institutional concepts, they are not truly creative leaders. There is perhaps no truer measure of a leader's greatness than the extent to which he succeeds in changing the ideas underlying old institutions. However, it should be noted that leaders rarely changed institutions as such. Leaders like Caesar, Jesus, and Ford who caused the emergence of new leadership classes did not actually change the institutions of government, religion, or enterprise. They gave them new interpretations and orientations, new scope and depth, new values and perspectives. The Roman imperial government was identified as being distinct from "barbarian" governments. Mass production and distribution are identified as being different from other methods of manufacturing, other means of distribution.

Briefly, institutions stand for principles of government, religion, enterprise, etc. Leadership classes represent specific interpretations of these principles. Heads of state cannot serve the interests of the people because, under the prevailing system, their primary loyalty must be to the nation. Dynamic leaders—Franklin D. Roosevelt, Lenin, etc.—are no exception; although they introduce new forms and ideas to existing institutions, they must give them an orientation, an identity distinct from and possibly opposed to the identities of others—as the ideology of the New Deal was opposed to that of the Economic Royalist, or that of the socialist differs from that of the communist. In either case, the people are relegated to and dependent upon the interests and policies as determined by the leadership class.

87

SUMMARY

The leadership class rises upon new opportunity, which may result from migration (as in the United States), war (Germany after the Franco-Prussian War of 1870-71), a revolutionary invention (the automobile), or a vision (the organized labor movement). Since opportunity is often the result of developing social forces (migration may result from oppression, war from expansion, an invention from a social need, a vision from exploitation), the rise of a leadership class is a dynamic development, riding upon the high tide of a movement that produces major changes.

When I previously stated that the importance of opportunity exists as much in its inception and incubation as in its ultimate realization, I was referring to the origin of new forms of government, new patterns of achievement, new means of creating wealth, new ways of life. The deeper significance of a new leadership class lies not so much in its being as in its becoming—and its departing. An example may illustrate the point.

The importance of the American leadership class that applied the principle of mass production and created, among others, the automobile industry lies not primarily in the fact that it produced and marketed millions of cars and thus put America on wheels. Its positive importance derives from the resonance of a vast continent binding together its teeming millions, from the dynamism of the economy and its technology, from the excited vision of a golden future that was practically at hand. Its negative importance lies in the fact that the era of that leadership has passed—resonance dulling into monotonous rhythm, dynamism freezing into a pattern, vision becoming near-sighted.

In a similar way, the significance of the age of electricity, starting with Edison, does not lie primarily in lighted streets and factories, in the introduction of a new kind of power into the economy, in the making of a new entertainment industry. Rather, its significance lies in the ability of a new leadership class to convert the dynamic power and enterprise of an aspiring nation into tangible values. The underground swell of new opportunity rather than the product in the store window is the factor responsible for the rise of a new leadership class.

For the people, too, the rise of a new class means change —though not necessarily for the better. If they think they are well off, as the people in the United States did after the

Second World War, they may be in for a severe shock. If they enjoy peace, as they did in the late thirties, war may just be around the corner. If they suffer from a prolonged depression, they will find a large measure of relief, as under Franklin D. Roosevelt. The early settlers in America were Spanish, French, and English subjects. They were replaced by American pioneers, hardy and independent. Later, more and more Americans became employees and dependent workers —dependent upon management, labor unions, and government. Now, they seem to be approaching a stage where they will become group individuals under state control.

The reason for the change in the status of the people is that every new leadership class represents a different identity, that is, it pursues a different set of interests. A leadership class cannot be identified without a distinctive orientation. In its practical application, distinctive orientation means rivalry (for power), competition (for markets), opposition (to policies), conflict (between dogmas), and war (between nations).

Disregarding the extent to which it may be employed, distinction is an indispensable principle in the life of groups and individuals. Without it, there is no meaning. However, if leadership classes differ from one another in the constant reaffirmation of their respective identities, why cannot the people do likewise?

Even if all the people on earth were of one kind and tied in close kinship, as they basically are, division on the leadership level would still compel profound divisions among them—as has been the case through the ages. Instead of being members of the human race first, people are Italians or Israelis first, Communists or Democrats first, Catholics or Buddhists first, bosses or workers first. The common basic human element is lost in the identifying cleavages among leadership classes. The basic interests of people and their basic right to live in dignity and economic security are subordinate to the priority of the distinctive identity determined by the special interests of leadership classes.

THE
LEADERSHIP
CLASS
AS
THE
RESULT
OF
SELECTION

In Chapter Two I had mentioned two major reasons for the inability of the people to benefit from expanding opportunity: a lack of broader interests and political indifference. This chapter will inquire further into these and related characteristics. The purpose is twofold : to better understand the people's behavior and attitudes, and to determine whether existing shortcomings can be remedied, at least in part.

Notwithstanding different standards of living in different countries, the people everywhere are prevented from developing interest and ability for the same reasons. Three of these reasons are physical needs, the need of protection, and fear.

PHYSICAL NEEDS AND INTELLIGENCE

Food and drink, sex, shelter, and clothing are among the prime physical essentials of people in any age and climate, in any type of economy and society, and under any form of government. In terms of a bowl of soup, a dish of rice, meat and potatoes, a glass of beer; in terms of a home to belong to, a bed or cot to sleep on; in terms of clothing for summer and winter; in terms of a mate to love, children to rear - in these and related terms one can speak of a "law of nature" of which no human being is exempt. While all persons are subject to these needs, not all persons respond to them in like fashion. To provide for them is of small concern to some. But to the people it generally is a full-time job, leaving neither time nor taste for such a demanding effort as acquiring an education or advancing themselves in other ways.

Those who disagree with the statement may point out that the present downward trend in working hours per week, to cite one example, gives the people more leisure, hence greater opportunity for education and training. However, getting an education requires more than extra time. Lacking material possessions, the people would have to work for an education, would have to accentuate certain interests, neglect or sacrifice others—among them perhaps a comfortable home life, relaxation, hobbies, or sports. They would need not only strong ambition, bold courage, and tough persistence but also the intelligence to see the long-term value of an education.

The requirements seem to lie beyond the statistical average. In a study, *Middletown,* made earlier in the century, Robert S. and Helen M. Lynd pointed out that most of the boys and girls stumbled on or fell into the particular jobs that became their life work. For the most part, they went to work by taking advantage of some vacancy they or their families happened to hear about and spent the rest of their lives doing this kind of work with whatever satisfaction it afforded. Out of each 100 engaged in earning a living, 85 worked for others and were closely directed by them. In 21 months, on the broad average, there was a chance for one person in 424 to be promoted.

Outside of working hours, people spent their time pleasantly enough; they danced, played cards, went for a ride or a hike. Some tinkered with their cars, tuned in their radios, tried out television sets; a few read books, more read magazines; others were interested in gardening and other hobbies.

The I.Q. percentage distribution of 667 children in all schools was as follows:[1]

Near genius	140 plus	0.2 per cent
Very superior	120–139	3.7
Superior	110–119	9.7
Average	90–109	52.6
Dull	80–89	21.0
Borderline, often feeble-minded	70–79	8.1
Moron	50–69	3.0
Imbecile	25–49	1.2
Idiot	below 25	0.5

As the survey was made in the United States before the Depression, it may be asked whether the statistical average has improved in any important degree since. If only 13.6 per cent of school children rated above average in intelligence then, how many do so today? How realistic is the expectation that general intelligence of children is sufficiently bright or their determination sufficiently strong to want to share in the advantages of the selective process of education? If this is a vital question in the United States, how is one to judge the chances of hundreds of millions of children living in less advanced countries in Asia, Africa, or Latin America? With relatively low standards of living, poor economic development, and limited communications and social contact, educational opportunities would be incomparably more difficult to realize.

There is a widespread belief that people are increasingly well educated and well informed. This belief is challenged by Michael Marien, a research fellow for the Syracuse University Research Corporation. He says that, on the contrary, as our society becomes more complicated and change occurs ever faster, people are in effect becoming more ignorant in terms of what they need to know.

Two conclusions seem to be indicated: first, it is unlikely

that the average intelligence among the school population in the United States has improved significantly over the last 30 to 40 years; and second, if the growing crisis is to be resolved, education on all levels must be radically restructured.[2]

PROTECTION

Although there are times, such as at the birth of the political collective, when the people provide their own protection, it is generally true that the satisfaction of physical needs compels them to seek protection. Regardless of time, place, or circumstance, the people depend upon others to provide the opportunities by which they can earn a living and possibly improve their lot. If these opportunities were not provided or were abused, the slaves would rise against their masters, the tenants against their lords, the peasants against their princes, and, in more recent times, the workers against their employers.

The importance of the principle of protection is shown by the fact that in the past virtually every ruler, from dictator to democrat, found it necessary to give primary attention to the physical needs of the people, regardless of his personal attitude. In our own age, the first legislation proposed by President Franklin D. Roosevelt dealt with effective measures to meet the physical needs of the people through jobs, loans, welfare, and other measures. One of the first acts signed by Adolf Hitler assured everyone a livelihood. Roosevelt and Hitler were sharply opposed on many basic principles, but the "principle" of providing for the needs of the people was equally important to both.

FEAR

The people's desire for protection has its origin in fear. Today, many people suffer hunger or are on the borderline of starvation. For them, starvation is an ever-present threat.

Then there are those who belong to the insecurity class. Their needs are above the grocery level but they lack the security provided by a savings account. Never secure, these people, again and again, must strive for an adequate living standard. Sometimes the result of a poor harvest or the ravages of fire, flood, or earthquake, more often insecurity is caused by the demands of a large family, sickness, the lack of providence, and the temptation to spend one's unstable income on things of fleeting value.

Then there are those among the people who suffer neither hunger nor economic insecurity but who live in fear of the specter of want. Not desperate, they are nonetheless desperately determined to keep want at a respectable distance. Fearful of the possible risk, they refrain from bold action in the economic struggle.

As a result, bold achievement, which is hardly ever without its temporary setbacks and never without sacrifice, is not attractive to the people. They prefer to hold on to their jobs because they cannot be sure how a change would turn out. Not infrequently they are promoted because they hide their true selves behind the screen of compliance. The attitude of the majority is basically negative; rather than considering what they might gain they dwell on what they might lose: job, savings, health and welfare benefits, pension, seniority rights.

These are some of the ties that bind the people to caution, habit, and conformity. The daily pressure of physical needs, the desire for protection, and the burden of fear, combined with other factors, prevent the people from trying for the uncommon achievement. They serve to make the people dependent upon others. These same reasons also prevent the people from developing an interest in things not connected with the immediate task of making a living, and from developing the ability to take advantage of opportunity.

How can it be shown that physical needs, need for protection, and fear impose this handicap upon the people; that, in a sense, they are responsible for the negative attitude? One way is to study the experience of those who seem to be relatively free from these needs and fears, those who have attained great leadership, outstanding achievement, or those who are generally known as "the great men." What is the attitude of great men toward physical needs, protection, fear, and want?

ATTITUDE OF THE "GREAT MAN"

Apart from the exceptions that confirm the rule, the outstanding man attaches little importance to any of the major motivations of the people. He is fairly free of the limitations they impose. As to physical needs, he is likely to make as light of them as possible. He usually has little or no fear because he neither seeks nor needs protection. The greatest use he makes of protection is to extend or to impose it upon others.

Disregard of physical needs may be shown by a few examples. Where most people like to sleep regular hours, many an outstanding man has done with a few hours of sleep at irregular intervals. Where most people like to keep an unruffled routine of work and play, the outstanding man often works fourteen, sixteen, eighteen hours at a time. Where most people are concerned with earning a livelihood, the outstanding man generally cares little for the weekly pay envelope as long as progress is being made toward the larger goal. Where the people consider a happy family life essential to their moral and material well-being, many an outstanding man or woman has subordinated family life to his or her aspirations.

This is not to say that all outstanding men sleep only a few hours every night, have no family life, know nothing but work, or go hungry for days. It may not be important that Napoleon slept only five hours a night, Edison even less. Important is the ability of these men to subordinate broad human habits to the concentrated drive of ambition. The workingman can skip a meal or a night's sleep if he is asked to. But the outstanding man will sacrifice food, sleep, the weekly pay, and other physical needs, sometimes to the limit of his endurance, not because he is told to but because he wants to.

There are, of course, many different views on the subject of leadership. Some speak of great men. as leaders; hence, they ascribe to them qualities of leadership. Speaking of the nature of leadership, Kimball Young says: "Leadership depends on attitudes and habits of domination in a few people and submissive behavior in others."[3] There are exceptions: neither Jesus nor Spinoza had "habits of domination." While great men lead others, outstanding achievement is not necessarily synonymous with leadership. It is possible to attain leadership without the concentration, devotion, and sacrifice mentioned before. "Leadership," says Young, "often arises out of crises." This may or may not apply to outstanding achievements. Discoveries (like Columbus'), conquests (like Pizarro's), and inventions (like Thomas Edison's and Henry Ford's) would be considered outstanding achievements but they bear no element of crisis.

Others deny the existence of basic leadership traits:

97

> This amounts briefly to a demonstration of the fact that leadership is a function of a definite situation and that we cannot talk about leadership traits in general but that instead we must talk about leadership traits in particular situations. We must talk about the traits of army leaders, the traits of student leaders, the traits of criminal leaders, the traits of political leaders, and so on always designating the leadership situation.[4]

These views emphasize important points, but it seems to me that, to have full significance, the points need to be seen and evaluated in their total perspective—the "Mankind perspective." This perspective would underline the fact that great men have basic traits in common without which outstanding achievement would hardly be possible.

One characteristic of the "great man" is the absence of fear. Either he is born without it, as Alexander the Great was said to be, or he is able to overcome it, as Goethe was. Pestalozzi was not afraid of his critics, nor Galileo of his persecutors, nor Jesus of his tormentors. Theodore Roosevelt did not tremble at the thought of losing an election, nor John Kennedy at the thought of having to fight a war, nor did

Thomas Jefferson hesitate before the task of penning an important document. Henry Ford did not worry over the size of his pay envelope, nor Benjamin Franklin over the loss of a job.

The great man in science and the arts—that is, the man who is not in public life—may not know fear because he is not concerned about physical needs. Again, the great man in public life may not know fear because he exploits it in others and may even help create it where it does not exist.

In ancient times, the great man created fear of spirits and gods. Today, he exploits and often creates or strengthens the fear of capitalism or communism, of the enemy abroad or the enemy at home, of the selfishness of management or the ruthlessness of labor, of Blacks or Jews, of unemployment, sickness, and old age. In the thirties, the conditions created by unemployment, closed banks, lost savings, inflation, and bread riots helped bring Franklin D. Roosevelt into power. While he warned that "the only fear we have to fear is fear itself," it is a matter of record that in subsequent years the fear of insecurity, the shadow of depression, the ghost of unemployment at home, and the threat of Franco, Mussolini, and Hitler abroad were important considerations in his government's policies and pronouncements. It is an open question whether Roosevelt would have been re-elected for a third and fourth term had he succeeded in putting an end to fear.

In times as tense and complex as ours, there is an abundance of fear. Hence, there is abundant opportunity for those who feel called upon to extend a protective hand. Even if there were no fear (a highly unlikely prospect), there would still be those, history shows, who would convince the people that they needed not only protection but, more importantly, needed *their* protection. It is not always relevant to their purpose whether such protection is needed or even wanted. This is the special domain of would-be dictators.

Some characteristics of the people would thus seem to form the basis of an attitude and, therefore, for a condition of dependence. Protection becomes the basic requirement on the one side and the foundation for leadership on the other.

Leaders must stress the need for protection or risk the loss of their following. Thus, political leaders emphasize the need for greater welfare (actually, there is no limit to "greater" welfare); social leaders stress the need for improving the lot of the people; labor leaders, the need to protect the worker against exploitation; and church leaders, the need for spiritual salvation. I emphasize this point not to cast doubt upon the validity of the claims made by the leadership but to show the important role fear plays in the relations between leadership and the people.

Yet there are those who belong neither to the great or to the people; their aspirations are not held down by the physical needs; they do not need protection, nor do they suffer fear or want. Is the connection between the outstanding achievement and freedom from want therefore merely a coincidence?

Hardly! The fact that one very large group with no outstanding achievement to its credit has practically all the characteristics of want and fear, while another very small group with the record of great achievement has few or none of them points to more than coincidence. It indicates that the outstanding achievement does not just happen but is the result of certain processes of preparation and selection that counteract needs and fears (either potential or real) such as those described above. I shall call these processes "the selective process."

In primitive as in advanced society, the selective process culminates in the "great man." He is defined as one who stands out among the masses (otherwise he could not be recognized) by the nature of his achievement (otherwise he could not be judged). The genius who is never heard from is thereby excluded. The term "great" is not meant to convey a judgment of quality. It is irrelevant to this discussion whether the achievement is "good" (Franklin D. Roosevelt) or "bad" (Adolf Hitler); whether it involves wealth (Andrew Carnegie), power (Napoleon), or influence (Thomas Jefferson); whether greatness is the result of ideas (Socrates) or deeds (Florence Nightingale); whether it is selfish (Caesar) or unselfish (Albert Schweitzer); whether it is based upon evaluation (Hegel) or application (Machiavelli); whether it takes the form of art (Wagner), science (Newton), politics (Lincoln), or economics (Marx).

SELECTION THROUGH EDUCATION

Education is the deliberate effort to acquire knowledge in order to advance oneself, not simply the process of going to school in obedience to the dictum of parents or teachers. Education may take the form of academic learning, diligent observation and analysis, self-learning, learning by inspiration and revelation, or knowledge may be acquired simply by experience. These methods of learning are available to anyone interested in acquiring an education. The difference in result lies in the intensity of learning and in the quality of the inquiring mind.

Wealth or, more precisely, a measure of financial security is related to education and leadership. Lester F. Ward points out that most of the heroes of Homer (who, it may be assumed, were "educated" men; they certainly were leaders) possessed great wealth consisting of thousands of heads of cattle, large numbers of slaves, and vast tracts of land. Unless they preferred poverty like Socrates, ancient philosophers either were independently wealthy like Plato or were sponsored by royalty or aristocrats who offered comfortable care of their personal wants and professional needs like Aristotle.

In the more recent days of the French Academy, it was found that of 100 foreign associates 41 belonged to the nobility or came from wealthy families; 52 were members of the middle class; 7 came from the working class. Of 36 French savants, 10 came from noble or wealthy families, 17 were members of the middle class and 9 belonged to the working class. More of these eminent men came from the smallest class (the wealthy) than from the largest (the workers), while the middle class accounted for the largest number.[5]

Alfred Odin arrives at similar findings. In a study of the careers of 619 distinguished men of letters spanning a period of 500 years, he found that 562, or 91 per cent, spent their youth in the absence of all material concern; the remaining 57, or 9 per cent, spent it in virtual poverty. In another study,[6] Odin noted that of 636 celebrated men of letters:

159	belonged to the nobility	or 25 per cent
187	were government officials	30
143	represented the professions	22
73	were of the bourgeoisie	11
61	were manual laborers	10

These findings indicate that financial independence, or at least a modicum of economic security, creates conditions conducive to intellectual achievement. The scholar whose material wants are taken care of has the choice of time, place, and subject for study. He can reflect leisurely. He can frequent places of inspiration and stimulation. He can buy books, select tools, acquire instruments, go to near and distant places for observation and experimentation—and do all these things without concern for food, shelter, or clothing. The advantage of economic security in the struggle of the mind is not to be denied.

This formula seems to apply with equal truth to those who achieve eminence in the affairs of state. Among the leaders of the English Revolution we find Oliver Cromwell, an East Anglian country gentleman; Henry Ireton, his son-in-law; Edmund Ludlow, the regicide, son of Sir Henry Ludlow of Wiltshire. The Leveler, John Lilburne, came from a family dating back to the fourteenth century. Robert Everard, leader of the Diggers and chronicled as "a gentleman of liberal education" was the son of an Anglican clergyman.[7]

Of the 56 persons who signed the Declaration of Independence, nearly all were affluent. Thirty-three had college degrees, not a mean distinction at the time. Of the 56:

---

22 were lawyers
11 were sons of ministers
11 were merchants
5 were physicians
4 were farmers
3 were ministers

Only four had little or no formal education.

Among the leaders of the French Revolution, we find the Duke of Orléans, cousin of the king; Mirabeau, the Lameths, and Lafayette, who were lawyers; Robespierre and Danton, of middle-class origin; Bailly, the astronomer; Lavoisier, the chemist; Monge, the mathematician; Brissot, Marat, and Desmoulins, the journalists; and Camus, the author, legal expert, and archivist.[8]

Over a hundred years later, the first Russian Revolution brought to the fore men like Milyukov, the historian from a distinguished family; Tereschenko, the sugar millionaire of Kiev; Guchkov, the wealthy Moscow merchant; the venerable Prince Lvov, scarcely less aristocratic among the Russians than the Feuillants were among the French or the Puritan Lords among the English.

The second Russian Revolution also featured the educated and the wealthy: Lenin, the son of a school inspector; Trotsky and Kamenev, both educated men; Dzerzhinsky, creator of the Cheka, of noble Polish-Lithuanian stock; Sverdlov, chemist by training; Stalin, student of the priesthood; Chicherin, the aristocrat.[9]

Speaking of the contemporary Chinese Revolution, Robert North says:

Although Chinese Communists hail their party as the vanguard of the proletariat, no Politburo member is known to have come from a working-class family. On the contrary, four admit wealthy landlord antecedents, one came from a line of small landlord officials, four class their parents as well-to-do landlords, and two emerged from the lesser peasantry. The social origins of two are uncertain. The educational level of these men is generally high. Nine have attended advanced institutions. [10]

SELECTION THROUGH INHERITANCE

A similar connection between the selective process and the outstanding person is found in inheritance. A study of one thousand gifted children in California revealed that 23, or about one in 40, were related to persons listed in *America's Hall of Fame.*[11] Apparently, one is more likely to become one of the select if one stems from the select. The far-reaching effect of sexual selection through inheritance is shown in the family tree which grew out of Richard Edwards' first marriage to Elizabeth Tuthill at Hartford, Connecticut, about three hundred years ago. Of their descendants:

1	was a U. S. Vice President
2	were U. S. Senators
3	were U. S. Congressmen
12	were college presidents
30	were judges
60	were prominent authors
60	were physicians
65	were college professors
75	were army officers
80	were government officials
100	were lawyers
100	were clergymen
265	were college graduates. [12]

Compare this record with the family tree of Max Juke, a

New England vagabond, born more than two hundred years ago. Of his descendants:

440	were wrecked by disease
310	were professional paupers
300	died in infancy
60	were thieves
50	were prostitutes
7	were murderers
53	were criminals of various classifications.[13]

While these are extreme examples, they indicate the long-range effect of inheritance upon eminence on the one side and degeneration on the other.

---

104 EMINENCE

The room for eminence is small. Since the dawn of history, eight or ten thousand years ago, some thirty billion persons have been reared to maturity in countries known to the historian. Eminence was reached by only about five thousand persons. At this rate, every six million members of the human race have reared on the average one to eminence. Of lesser talents, it has been estimated, there were perhaps 125,000, or one in a quarter million.[14]

Even among those who are practically born to eminence, genius is rare. A study of 823 royal persons over a period of 500 years of European history shows only about 20 who possessed the genius of Frederick the Great, Peter the Great, Gustavus Adolphus, William the Silent, or Eugene of Savoy. This is a ratio of one in 40. In contrast, England, France, and Germany, with a history of far more than 500 years and each with many millions of inhabitants, have not produced more than 200 men of such unquestioned genius—a rate of considerably less than one in a million. [15]

DEGENERATION

As genius represents the highest development among outstanding men, so another type represents the corresponding extreme among the people—the frustrated, hopeless, desperate person. Max Juke is an extraordinary example of human degeneration. Not many people are like Max Juke. But neither could many people be found who, exposed to similar poverty and disease, would escape similar misfortune. Pursued by failure, stricken by physical or mental illness, suffering from lack of emotional balance, many of these unfortunates will turn to alcohol or other temporary relief. Evidently, the imaginary world produced by the magic of alcohol, looks more inviting than the one in which these people are compelled to carry on their feeble struggle.

OTHER VIEWS

The principle of selection, as interpreted here, represents only one opinion. There are many others. Dr. Horace Mann Bond, then Dean of Education at Atlanta University, wrote in 1960:

> I believe that potentially high intellectual ability is not rare, nor to be found only in a select and limited group of human beings; on the contrary, I believe that there is an enormous reservoir of high potential abilities in our population that now, for all practical purposes, goes to waste.

After a brief critical review of the writings of Sir Francis Galton who held "that eminent 'men of science' and of other fields derived from relatively few family lines," he concluded:

> In brief: our argument is that, could we but give to every child in the land the same opportunities for intellectual stimulation now enjoyed by the children of professional, technical and kindred workers, we could increase our "talent pool" fivefold. Even if we

could move but part-way in this direction, as suggested by our medium estimate, we could have available more than 80,000 "talents" in place of our presently estimated 28,000. The measure of future potential would be even greater, for the elevation of the entire community would inevitably raise the standard, by increasing the proportion of "talented" to be derived from the top class. [16]

I readily agree that broader and better education would produce a higher percentage of talented persons. This applies as much to the United States and other democratic countries as to the Soviet Union and other communist countries, and probably as much to formal as to informal education. The revolutionary phase through which many of the developing nations in Asia, Africa, Latin America are passing seems to afford an unrivalled opportunity, an improved education in these countries offers a most effective method of discovering talented persons.

But while the discovery of new talent would help individuals, nations, cultures, and civilization itself, it does not necessarily mean that it would change the basic relationship between leaders and people nor the basic and traditional role of the people in society. The determining factor in maintaining that relationship is not the quantity of talent but the quality of leaders. The emergence of the latter, in turn, may depend more upon the dynamic changes of the times than upon the methods of finding new talent, at least under the existing societal system.

Describing the relation between society and individuals, Arnold Toynbee says:

Society is a "field of action" but the *source* of all action is in the individuals composing it. This truth is forcibly stated by Bergson:

"We do not believe in the 'unconscious' (factor) in history: 'the great subterranean currents of thought,' of which there has been so much talk, only flow in consequence of the fact that masses of men have been carried away by one or more of their own number . . . . It is useless to maintain that (social progress) takes place of itself, bit by bit, in virtue of the spiritual condition of the society at a certain period of its history. It is really a leap forward which is only taken when the society has made up its mind to try an experiment; this means that the society must have allowed itself to be convinced, or at any rate allowed itself to be shaken; and the shake is always given by *somebody*.[17]

These individuals who set going the process of growth in the societies to which they "belong" are more than mere men. They can work what to men seem miracles because they themselves are superhuman in a literal and no mere metaphorical sense.[18]

CHAPTER
SEVEN

IS THE
FUTURE LIKELY
TO CHANGE
THE PRINCIPLES
OF EXPLOITATION?

The select group, represented by the "great man," has historically been comprised largely of those who have suc-ceeded most signally in acquiring wealth, power, and influ-ence. In other words, those who acquired these assets were distinguished by the greatest ability to acquire them. Or expressed still more directly: those who acquired these assets were the only members of the human race who could have acquired them.[1]

No one has yet been able to say precisely what causes one person to emphasize certain values or what gives him the ability to devote his life to their attainment. A combination of factors is necessary to realize the given potentials of one person. These circumstances may create only one Christ, one Disraeli, one Henry Ford, one Karl Marx, one Albert Ein-stein. Evidently, the combination is rare.

The fact that the process of selectivity has been operating throughout human history suggests that the phenomenon may be beyond man's control. Could it be that the "great man" is created by natural forces and that there may be one purpose in his creation and another in the creation of the people?

SELECTIVITY

The principle of selectivity, of course, is not confined to the human race. Both human and non-human species develop according to principles of selection. Charles Darwin showed the importance of natural selection for all the species. Julian Huxley stated that "not only is natural selection inevitable, not only is it *an* effective agency of evolution, but it is *the* only effective agency of evolution."[2]

But while the principle of selection applies to both human and non-human species, the purpose differs in each case. In the non-human species, natural selection serves to adapt the species to a certain way of life for the purpose of survival. In the human species, natural selection became social selection when the species developed a new pattern of organized living. Cassirer says:

> Man has, as it were, discovered a new method of adapting himself to his environment. Between the receptor system and the effector system, which are to be found in all animal species, we find in man a third link which we may describe as the *symbolic* system. This new acquisition transforms the whole of human life.[3]

At this point in the course of social development, the processes of social selection tend to endanger rather than to insure the species' survival. Along with love, compassion, and cooperation, the human society has generated discrimination, conflict, and hostility in ever rising measure. Does this development indicate that the advance of civilization may have taken place at the risk of survival? Selection has an important meaning for the individual person as well as for nations, races, and other groups and classes, but should it not also have a meaning for humanity as a whole—for the survival of the species? If it has such a meaning, how are we to understand the processes of selection which seem to endanger this survival? If it has not, and if such meaning is indispensable to the survival of the species, how could it be created?

Scientists have warned against the blind acceptance of natural selection:

> Man has reached a solitary pinnacle of evolutionary success by having evolved a novel method of adapting to the environment—that by means of culture. Having ventured on this biological experiment, our species cannot any longer rely entirely on forces of natural selection as they operate on the biological level. Man must carefully survey the course that lies ahead and constantly study his genetic progress. He can then prepare to take over the controls from Nature if it should become necessary to correct the deficiencies of natural selection. Only thus can he insure for himself continued evolutionary advance.[4]

Thinking in a similar vein, modern economists have pointed out that it is entirely within the reach of society to free men everywhere from the burden of physical needs and the fears attached to them. If it were possible to establish control of natural selection and to eliminate the burden of physical needs, would this not bring about a profound change in human relationships, especially in those between the people and their leaders?

111

I believe that the answer is in the negative. Forms, methods, and expressions have undergone many changes during the existence of the human race. Fears based on superstition have given way to fears based on insecurity, illness, and old age. Needs for roots and berries have been replaced by needs for canned and frozen foods. The "symbolic" system, which only man seems to have developed, has refined, enlarged, and intensified social relationships. However, the system has not altered the basic relationships. While forms, methods, and expressions have undergone many changes, the principles upon which social relationships are based have remained unchanged.

The apparent reason is that the changes have always taken place within an unchanging societal framework. They have never gone beyond the limits of the human society. Whether or not they could have done so is something else. They have never affected the basic relationships within that framework, especially that between the people and their leaders. The great religions, institutions, cultures, and governmental systems have usually taken this basic relationship for granted, partly because it has always existed, partly because there was no alternative. Thus, any refinements of one side equally affect the other. A few examples may illustrate the point.

As the people gain a higher standard of living, leadership advances the use of technological devices like mass production. As standards of living rise due to mass production, leadership introduces still more advanced technological devices such as automation. As standards continue to rise, . . . and so the cycle goes on. Or with regard to communication: as the people come into closer contact with their society, leadership uses better means of communication such as the printed word. As the people gain better education, leadership uses more advanced means of communication: radio and television, audio-visual devices, and paperbacks. As the people try to keep up with the news in a society that is steadily growing more complex, leadership introduces still more advanced forms of communication such as mass propaganda, psychological induction methods, and perhaps brainwashing.

Through all these improvements, leadership keeps ahead of the people who in turn readily follow leadership. The basic relationship between the two remains unchanged. It would seem logical to conclude that as long as that relationship continues to operate under essentially the same societal system, any future improvements are unlikely to affect the basic relationship between the people and leadership.

ABOLITION OF WAR

The most powerful instrument of exploitation of the people is war. Among the reasons that it is such an effective tool are:

(1) The reality or even the threat of war places the people in a position in which they are confronted with an absolute dictum: they *must* go to war if so ordered; they *must*

sacrifice opportunity, career, family, and life itself if so instructed; they *must* do as told—with few or no questions asked.

(2) War being an emergency, it dominates not only the lives of the people, their aspirations, their hopes, and their relationships, it dominates everything else—the body politic, the economic system, and the social life.

(3) War plays into the hands of the leadership class, which can have practically any law enacted, any measure adopted, any order carried out, because the purpose of the emergency is to win the war—and only the leadership can win it.

These reasons are not cited to imply a moral judgment but merely to emphasize the power of war as an instrument of exploitation.

Obviously, one of the most effective ways of combating exploitation would be to abolish war. But would it not also appear that, since war is such a powerful tool in the hands of the leadership class, it is essential to progress? Two somewhat extreme schools of thought (extreme for the purpose of clarity) may be presented:

(1) There can be no real progress for the people as long as there is war.

(2) There can be no real progress if war is abolished.

Let us look at the second statement first. War can hardly be considered indispensable to progress. Most human progress has been made in times of peace. Great and basic changes have sometimes been fostered by war but that does not mean they might not have taken place in the absence of war. The abolition of slavery, the organized labor movement, and the emancipation of women are milestones on the road of progress; so are Confucianism, Buddhism, Judaism, Christianity, Islam, and other religions. One of the world's great war lords, Emperor Asoka of India, abolished war altogether, putting in its place a policy of peace, enlightenment, and love.

Noted scholars such as Pitirim Sorokin have pointed out that the qualities of love and altruism have proved of far greater significance in the life of the human society than the qualities of hatred and enmity, that the instrument of peace is of far greater importance than the instrument of war.[5]

It may well be possible to explain the abolition of slavery, the organized labor movement, the emancipation of women, as well as the origin of the great religions, without reference to war. However, many of the important changes and major improvements, including the great religions, sprang from catastrophes in which war played a major role.[6]   Not a few of the most ardent religious believers (crusaders and conquerors, popes and princes, kings and emperors) have used war as an instrument to further their spiritual devotion.

Love and altruism have played and are playing a most important role in the history of human society, but they have not proved decisive in its evolution and development. Why, if they are the dominant trait in human nature, have they not had more effect? Thinkers and scholars have not provided conclusive evidence or explanation. In the absence of such evidence, what gives us the right to assume that the forces of love and altruism can prevail now where they have never prevailed before? Must we not find out first of all why they have failed in the past?

Asoka was indeed a great ruler and a great man, but in all history he seems to have been one of the very few military monarchs who abandoned warfare after victory. Rather than a shining example of the power of love, is he not the rare exception? What justifies the expectation that the exceptional deeds of a single person can be transformed into a moral code guiding the actions of many people?

In order to evaluate the quality as well as the importance of love in its true significance, it is necessary to consider both sides. The child needs love for basic nourishment but it also needs to assert its individual traits. Cooperation is important, but the recognition of personal aspirations is no less significant. Love is a deep and basic urge, but other drives are as deep and as basic: hunger, ambition, and loyalty to the family, the community, the race, the nation, or the church.

Those who believe that war can be abolished as an instrument of human relations will find little encouragement and less support in the history of past millennia. Let those who speak glibly of the abolition of war ponder some of the difficulties that would be created under the present societal system. Let those who want to correct the processes by which leadership classes rise and fall show how to control the forces responsible for the powerful fluctuations in human societies.

Let us assume that, in the absence of a supernational authority, the nations of the world would agree to abolish war. There would be neither economic nor political exploitation by the victors of the last war; no expanding markets; no extended spheres of political influence; neither territorial acquisitions by force nor postwar use, direct or indirect, of the military power which had won the last war.

Even if the victors of the last war were willing to make these and other concessions, it would still be necessary to make the vanquished promise not to take advantage of the self-sacrifice on the part of the victors, not to seek revenge, not to rebuild military power or seek compensation for damages suffered; not to sell or to out-bargain the former enemy or other nations in such a way that economic rivalry again might lead to war.

And this is not all! Apart from complete disarmament, a system would have to be set up that would effectively prevent the threat of war—a system by which discoveries would be controlled or perhaps suppressed or destroyed so as not to cause harm to any nation or people; by which standards of production would be geared to standards of consumption; by which industries would grow without tariff protection; by which population as well as migration would be held to agreed-upon limits; by which the land would be opened to all people because to keep them out might lead to overpopulation, violence, and war. In the absence of a world authority, these goals seem unattainable.

Suppose we consider war as nature's means of being fruitful—fruitful in the dynamic sense. Since war is (or used to be) fruitful in its victorious and its catastrophic aspects, nature need not progress any further in this direction. However, for man's purposes, it is not enough that war is merely fruitful. It must be fruitful to someone. Here enters the subjective distinction: war becomes an instrument of human aspirations. It operates as the great lever which tears old nations loose and raises others in their place. It dethrones old leaderships and elevates new classes. It becomes the promoter of large-scale aspirations.

It also keeps the different factions of mankind effectively apart in alert opposition. New leadership classes rise not only upon the general opportunities created by war, they also take advantage of the *special* opportunity to act against other leadership classes and, therefore, against other nations: Communist China against Soviet Russia, the Arab states against Israel, the new African nations against the old Western powers.

The instrument of war has thus created divided loyalties and competing aspirations. It would thus seem realistic to expect that war could be abolished if an equally effective instrument, for example world government, were created to replace it.

NUCLEAR WAR

Does this interpretation of the role of war in human history apply to the modern age? Does not the character of nuclear war create an entirely new pattern of relationships between nations? Wars in our century have meant victory for some nations and defeat for others, the loss of several million human lives, and the destruction of property running into hundreds of billions of dollars. Nuclear war, it is asserted, would mean the end of Western, perhaps of all civilization, even the end of the human race. If the principles of national rivalry and competing ideologies represented by leadership classes were responsible for wars in the past, have they not lost validity before the cataclysmic consequences of a possible nuclear war?

These and related questions should be answered in the negative. One reason is that weapons of defense are likely to catch up with weapons of aggression; they always have. The principles that have been valid throughout history are not likely to lose their validity two-thirds through the twentieth century. Armor caught up with powder; the phalanx with the cavalry; the trench with the tank. It is unlikely that new principles created by nuclear fission will prevent future scientists from discovering means or methods of minimizing or nullifying the effects of hydrogen bombs, intercontinental missiles, and even more hideous weapons of attack. The fact that we do not know today just what form these defensive instruments and weapons will take must not cause us to say with finality: "Impossible!"

Another reason lies in the historical experience: sheer terror has yet to prevent any major war. Some degree of terror, it is safe to say, has accompanied the introduction of every major weapon of attack—from Hannibal's elephants to dynamite, the U-boat, massive bombing, chemical warfare, and the atom bomb. In the light of history, it is a grievous mistake to assume that the terrifying prospect of nuclear war will prevent nuclear war.

Still another reason is that the people have no real control over issues of war and peace. Even if they are sufficiently agitated to wish to break all political and social restraints, the people will nonetheless serve the institutions to which they and their leaders have sworn loyalty. If a major foreign power threatened the American way of life, would not the American people support their government and, if need be, go to war—H-bomb or no H-bomb? Would not the Russian or the Chinese or, for that matter, any people do likewise? Are not the leaders of nations bound in loyalty to defend the system they represent? How, then, can hundreds of millions of angry people rise in righteous indignation and demand their governments to stop all this tragic waste and misery?

Inasmuch as the arguments against nuclear war can thus be seen to rest upon erroneous assumptions, we can conclude that the arrival of the atomic age has caused no basic change in the principles responsible for past wars. I, therefore, believe that under the prevailing societal system there will probably be one or more atomic wars. The wars will occur as soon as one or more of the aggressive powers develops weapons of defense to a point that their ruling powers consider war a justifiable risk.

It is correct to evaluate war and economic opportunity in contemporary as well as in future ages in terms of the prevailing principles of the past. Then as now, the greatest leadership class can arise only on the strength of the greatest opportunity. Then as now, war can create that opportunity most effectively. Then as now, only war can do away with old forms of political organization, such as nations, putting in their place new forms, such as a Western Alliance, a Soviet Bloc, or whatever. Only a basic reorientation and radical reorganization of man's existing societal system, featuring the establishment of a world authority under a world law, could effectively change these principles.

CHAPTER EIGHT

THE
MIDDLE
CLASS

This story of "the people" is hardly complete if it is
confined to an outstanding person on the one side and to the
people on the other. A substantial part of the world's population belongs to neither group, but forms another and very
important segment—"the middle class."

In preceding chapters it was shown that the people are
instrumental in creating new opportunity and that the leadership class is instrumental in exploiting it. The gap between
the high talents of the leaders and the dependence of the
people is obviously much too wide to permit effective economic and political organization and, therefore, a balanced
societal relationship. That gap is filled by the middle class.

DEFINITION AND IDENTITY

Perhaps the simplest way to define the middle class is to
say that its members have qualities not common among
either the people or the leaders. Generally, they are not
dependent upon others for a livelihood, as are the people, nor

are they particularly qualified, by ability or aspiration, to lead others in the organization and exploitation of substantial new opportunity, as are leaders. This characterization differs from the usual definition of the lower classes as being poor, the upper classes as being rich, and the middle class as being in between.

The criterion applied here is not exclusively one of economic success and accompanying social status. It is rather a combination of socio-economic status and intellectual equipment. Only in this way can the relationship of the middle class to the people on the one side and to the leadership class on the other be determined. A carpenter sometimes belongs to the leadership class (Jesus), sometimes to the middle class (as often in the United States), sometimes to the people. A lawyer is found sometimes in the leadership class (Lincoln), mostly in the middle class, and occasionally among the people. It is therefore inadvisable to use economic class distinction as a criterion.

Whereas (in the established nation) the people have small economic resources and in general depend upon employment by others for their livelihood, the middle class has greater economic freedom, and is often able to choose between taking employment, being self-employed, or giving employment to others. Whereas the people have little inclination to comprehend the intricacies of politics and economics, of social forces, cultural patterns, and the many factors that affect their lives, the middle class is more discriminating. Whereas the people are instrumental (by means of a high birth rate, for example) in creating the social climate and economic opportunity, the middle class has definite ideas about such things as birth control.

Whereas the leadership class is important because of its ability to develop new opportunity and to pave the way for the creation of wealth and power on a substantial scale, the middle class can neither develop the one nor pave the way for the creation of the other without the direction of the leadership class.

The fact that the middle class is not characterized by

leadership qualities does not mean that it is meek and afraid to move. Far from it! Members of the middle class have often put up a stubborn fight whenever property, opportunity, or personal liberty are threatened. In every major revolution, including the Russian Revolution which banished all three classes, members of the middle class have not remained silent. However, whereas the leadership class is highly dynamic in bringing about major change, the middle class does tend toward a functional role in society. It keeps the system operating. In contrast, the leadership class keeps expanding the system, pushing it to operate on a faster and larger scale.

Property is the principal interest of the middle class; this has tended to make it conservative. Although it strives to add to its possessions, its primary concern is to preserve them. The greater its possessions, the more pronounced its conservatism. Identification with property gives the middle class its basic character as well as its importance throughout the history of the human society. From Lucius Annaeus Seneca to Lewis Henry Morgan, social thinkers have held that the development of civilization is based upon the concept of property as it evolved to ever greater refinement and complexity. If property is the backbone of civilization, the middle class is the backbone of property.

It may be thought that, as members of the middle class help build cities, expand commerce, develop arts and sciences, further education, promote religion, and keep increasing the nation's wealth and power, they thereby create new economic and other opportunity. Actually, the middle class does not *create* new opportunity, at least not as we have defined it. The middle class elaborates, intensifies, and refines opportunity; in contrast, members of the leadership class create original opportunity—by discovering new land (Columbus), new tools (Watt), new methods (Ford), or new ideas (Gandhi).

Important as it is for the development of political groups, the middle class is not as indispensable as the people and the leaders are. Groups can and do exist without a middle class, as witnessed by many tribes living under primitive conditions with leaders and people, but without a middle class. In the past, organized groups, which eventually became city-states and nations, initially had no middle class, only leaders and people. Isolated nations, such as Japan and Russia were for centuries, had only a small middle class.

ECONOMIC OPPORTUNITY

Often small or absent in the early stages, the middle class develops rapidly in the expanding economy. The established nation always has a middle class, and the advanced nation has a large middle class in proportion to its population. The growth of the middle class begins with the opportunity afforded by dynamic group activity. Primitive tribes rarely carry on such activity; young states and nations generally have yet to develop it.

Like the leadership class, the middle class is a product of economic opportunity. The leadership class responds to opportunity as soon as it appears: newly conquered territory such as the American colonies, a newly developed device such as the machine, a novel idea such as Christianity. In contrast, the growth of the middle class depends upon the organization and initial development of new opportunity. In established states and nations, the middle class has readily exploited economic opportunity. In advanced states and nations, it has derived substantial gains from it over a long period of time and has attained growth, wealth, political power, and international recognition.

Throughout the ages, the middle class has developed as a result of economic opportunity. For centuries, ancient Greece had no middle class. As her maritime trade grew, "men who could never have hoped for wealth as farmers, grew rich. A new class arose, who made much money in trade, a middle class, neither nobles nor peasants."[1] Once economic opportunity existed, the growth of the middle class was assured together with its contributions to the growing power and influence of Greece. The middle class played an important part in the development of foreign commerce after military victories had paved the way. In ancient Rome, merchants of the middle class followed the same pattern after the legions had smashed their way through the established order. In neither Greece nor Rome could the fruits of military conquest have yielded an equally rich and enduring return without the ingenuity and industry of the middle class.

The age of mercantilism also was brought about by the middle class which, in the thirteenth century, dominated the commerce of the Mediterranean and the Adriatic. Venetian ducats and Florentine florins were then the standard coins of Europe.[2]

Evidence of the vital role of the middle class appeared in other parts of Europe. The Gothic cathedral, a monument to the power and wealth of guild craftsmen, was originally designed to take the place of civic buildings and to house the activities of prosperous towns. The Church, which then took part or at least an interest in practically every kind of commercial enterprise, occupied the choir. Other activities took place in transept and nave: trade and manufacture, bakery and butchery, plays and letterwriting, even military affairs. At that stage of political development, the cathedral reflected an important economic role played by the thriving middle class.[3]

Centuries later the steam engine produced an avalanche of new economic opportunity, which once more gave powerful impetus to the growth of middle classes all over Europe.

POLITICAL OPPORTUNITY

If economic opportunity promoted the origin and early growth of the middle class, political opportunity helped it to maturity, power, and influence. Class conflict accompanied the middle class from the start. Ludwig Gumplowicz says that the earliest class conflicts were the struggle for adjustment between the sovereign and the subject classes. This relatively simple process was soon interrupted, however, by the development of a class of foreign merchants which marked the emergence of what was to become an important element in every population: the middle class or bourgeoisie.[4]

Frederick L. Schuman refers thus to political interests and activities of nineteenth—century middle classes:

> *Fraternité*, no less than *Liberté* and *Egalité*, was the battle cry of the bourgeois revolution. And as nationalism is always bred of war, the impact of people upon people in the great Napoleonic conflicts intensified national consciousness at the very time when the bourgeoisie was rising to grasp power from kings and aristocrats. The revolutions of the mid-century were led and supported by middle-class patriots for whom the achievements of national unity and of democratic constitutionalism were but two facets of the same liberal program. The tide of nationalism in almost every State rose in proportion to the economic and political ascendancy of the bourgeoisie.[5]

Enterprising though it is, the middle class is not imbued with a pioneer spirit. Generally, it does not swing into action until the opportunity for profit or gain is clearly established. Each forward step is taken only after the new ground has been tested—often by others. But once the forward step has been decided upon, the middle class fights for it consistently and stubbornly. Frequently, it does so in the name of progress, sometimes for the benefit of the people:

> The middle class was the first to make the appeal to "universal human rights, to freedom and equality." It pretended to be interested in advancing the interests of the masses and thus gained their support. While the masses were not rewarded to the extent of the promises made by the middle class, they gained experience in the methods of carrying on the struggle for political emancipation.[6]

Its progressive attitude has often brought the middle class into conflict with the ruling powers. Harry Elmer Barnes points to the impact of the commercial revolution:

> The increased numbers, power, and ambition of the new middle class produced by the commercial revolution brought them into conflict with the absolute monarchs, who tried to tax and restrict the trade of the merchants in an arbitrary manner. In order to justify bourgeois resistance, the theory of natural rights, the

social contract, and the right of revolution were most convenient and appropriate. [7]

Through the centuries, the middle class continued the struggle for political power:

> The German middle class was twice defeated in its fight for political power: in the premature revolution of 1848 and during the struggle between Bismarck and the Prussian parliament over the control of the army in the sixties. Bismarck's empire represented a working compromise between the Junkers and the bourgeoisie. [8]

The history of the middle class is an odd mixture of tough opposition and ready compromise. "The middle class, in its attempt to keep its economic and social position, has been as enthusiastic about fascism as the industrialists have." [9] Sometimes, its basic conservatism places it in a position where it opposes both the government and the people. William Graham Sumner speaks of "Forgotten Men" who make up that great self-respecting middle class in society:

> Being industrious, independent, and unobtrusive, this class attracts little attention, but, in reality, it is incomparably the most important of all social classes in its contribution to every phase of civilization.
>
> While this middle class never asks for any assistance from the government for itself, it invariably has to defray a disproportionate share of the expense of every extension of state activity: It's the 'Forgotten Man' who is threatened by every extension of the paternal theory of government. It is he who must work and pay. When, therefore, the statesmen and social philosophers sit down to think what the State can or ought to do, they really mean to decide what the Forgotten Man shall do.
>
> The expense which is inherent in every extension of state activity always falls upon the middle class, but this class gets little or no benefit from these added burdens and tends to be crushed or diminished by them. Inasmuch as this class is, beyond all comparison, the most important element in the population, any extension of state action tends to menace the most valuable group in society for the benefit of those whose very need of assistance marks them off as inferior. [10]

The shifting attitudes and policies of the middle class have been severely criticized, among others by Auguste Comte. Says Harry Elmer Barnes:

> He was witnessing the disintegration of the old social order, as a result of the French and the industrial revolutions, and was keenly conscious of the evils of the new, though still transitional, society . . . Comte joined with Sismondi in condemning the new capitalistic order . . .

Comte's point of view was thus stated by Lucien Lévy-Bruhl:

> Comte saw the bourgeoisie at work during Louis Phillippe's reign, and he passes severe judgment upon it. Its political conceptions, he says, refer not to the aim and exercise of power, but especially to its possessions. It regards the revolution as terminated by the establishment of the parliamentary regime, whereas this is only an "equivocal halting-place." A complete social reorganization is not less feared by this middle class than by the old upper classes. Although filled with the critical spirit of the eighteenth century, even under a Republican form it would prolong a system of theological hypocrisy by means of which the respectful submission of the masses is insured, while no strict duty is imposed upon the leaders. This is hard upon the proletariat, whose condition is far from improving. It "establishes dungeons for those who ask for bread." It believes that these millions of men will be able to remain indefinitely "encamped" in modern society without being properly settled in it with definite and respected rights. The capital which it holds in its hands, after having been an instrument of emancipation, has become one of oppression. It is thus that, by a paradox difficult to uphold, the invention of machinery, which *a priori* one would be led to believe, would soften the condition of the proletariat, has, on the contrary, been a new cause of suffering to them, and has made their lot a doubly hard one. Here, in brief, we have a formidable indictment against the middle classes, and in particular against the political economy which has nourished them.[11]

126

DECLINE

As the nation begins to lose power and importance, the middle class as a whole loses the spirit of toughness and enterprise that marked its earlier course. At such times, the demand for security, social and otherwise, is loud and persistent; protection is the motto of the day. The English middle class of the twentieth century, with its emphasis on protection by the state and security against the hazards of life, is a far cry from the spirit and enterprise shown by the middle class two and three centuries before, when it first triumphed over what H.G. Wells calls "the dreams and schemes of Machiavellian absolutism,"[12] and later succeeded in building the empire.

The middle class develops because of expanding economic opportunity engendered by political organizations (city, state, nation). Its decline concurs with their decline. The end of the Greek city-states marked the end of the economic importance of the middle class, but not the end of its existence. Descendants of members of the middle class continued to manufacture and trade their wares in Greek cities. Others moved to more promising markets: Alexandria, Babylon, Byzantium, Carthage, Pergamum, Rhodes, Sidon, and Tyre. Still others gave up the struggle for an independent existence, moving back into the ranks of the people. The middle class lost its identity within the political group (city or state), but its members retained in large measure the identity of their craft or trade, with some change in locality. This shift occurred in ancient economies (Egypt, Babylonia, Greece, Rome, Carthage) as well as in medieval ones (Florence and Venice).

However, the situation of modern political groups is different. For one thing, earlier middle classes were never as large and as complex as they are in modern developed nations as a result of industrialism and economic opportunities created by it. Whereas a leadership class may disappear (and usually does) if unable to meet the challenge of new economic opportunity, the middle class survives. A possible reason is that modern nations do not perish as ancient empires did. When a modern nation, like Czechoslovakia, loses its independence, it may re-emerge in a new alignment, such as the Soviet bloc. Perhaps some day, Czechoslovakia will be a Western democracy again, but in the meantime its middle class continues to exist—if within a different economic and political framework.

127

THE
MIDDLE
CLASS
IN
AMERICA

EVOLUTION

The evolution of the middle class in America is a special case in history. Americans did not start from scratch. Many of the early immigrants were of the middle class. The American political and economic collective began as a middle-class entity rather than as a group of leaders and people. America is probably one of the few nations that began largely as a middle class, dividing later into the people and a leadership class, with the middle class holding its own. This evolution is possible in modern times; often members of the middle class of an advanced country migrate to newer countries. In contrast to ancient and medieval times, modern nations can and do begin their existence with some kind of a middle class. In Ghana and Nigeria and in Indonesia and Algeria, a middle class was present from the very beginning, although its strength may not have been equal to that of early America or modern Israel.

In early America, the opportunity for all to gather wealth on a substantial scale made from the beginning for an exceptionally dynamic concept of enterprise. The colonists did not live the sealed-off and rather stagnant life of the European peasant. Nor were they chained to a tradition inherited from countless generations living on the same land. Says Charles Beard:

> The overwhelming majority of the emigrants to America were from the "middling orders"—agricultural, mercantile, and artisan. Wrote Mercy Otis Warren, herself a colonial, born in 1728:

> "The first emigrations to North America were not composed of a strolling banditti of rude nations, like the first people of most other colonies in the history of the world. . . ."

> The early settlers in the newly discovered continent were as far advanced in civilization, policy, and manners; in their ideas of government, the nature of compacts, and the bands of civil union, as any of their neighbors at that period among the most polished nations of Europe. . . .[1]

> Of the 750,000 people who migrated to America between 1600 and 1770, about two thirds belonged to families able to pay for the crossing from Europe and to make a start of some kind in the new country. The other third, although lacking in money or property, had skills and talents which they could apply in earning a living (they were indentured servants).[2]

From the beginning, the immigrants made the most of the extraordinary opportunities they found practically everywhere in the new land.

> Most of the immigrants knew more about agriculture than about any other practical art. In Europe they had been accustomed to the production of a few standard commodities—grains, fruits, vegetables, meats. In the colonies, due to the variations in climate and soil, they were able to produce new and special crops. This fact had a decisive influence on the branches of agriculture which they developed, on types of commodities entering into the trade with the mother country, on the growth of wealth in America, and on the social characteristics from Maine to Georgia.[3]

What was true of agriculture was equally true of manufacturing and many other fields of endeavor. Consider the case (by no means unique) of Samuel Slater. He had serious difficulty introducing his cotton-spinning machine in America because English laws barred him from taking his drawings out of the country. Eventually, he designed them from memory. In 1791, Slater put a spinning mill in operation in Rhode Island. In 1807, only 15 cotton mills existed in the country, operating 8,000 spindles. At this point, members of the middle class began to take notice. Four years later, the number of mills had increased to 87, the number of spindles to 80,000. After another four years, and with the opportunities beyond reasonable doubt, more than 500,000 spindles were in operation.[4]

THE UNIQUE OPPORTUNITY

In the context of this book, Samuel Slater would be called a "leader," the operators who followed his lead would be called "members of the middle class." Slater's experience, which was repeated *ad infinitum* in American history, underlines the unique opportunity confronting the members of the middle class, natives and immigrants alike, in every field of endeavor, in every part of the expanding country. This opportunity differed greatly from the European experience and was not to be equaled anywhere in the world for a long time.

The opportunity was unique because America offered conditions of space, climate, natural resources, and, later, of population, trade, industry, and society, that were entirely different from those of Europe. An example is the development of the automobile. Its original invention was made in Europe, but the wide expanse of Europe was cut into small pieces by the rivalry and hostility of competing nations. The unlimited capability of the mechanical tool was held in check and condemned to temporary frustration by the pettiness of the human mind.

Neither the incentive to release the spirit of human adventure, nor the motivation to build cars for millions of people eager to see the world, nor the prospect of building chains of profitable service stations was enlisted in support of the

European market. Limitations of borders, jealousies of politicians, and scores of other barriers delayed the development of the automobile industry, and with it boundless opportunity. America had none of the limitations and all of the attractions. Leaders like Henry Ford saw the opportunity. Members of the middle class—entrepreneurs, investors, speculators, manufacturers, engineers, merchants—saw it, used it, refined it, and exploited it.

MIDDLE CLASS AS REFINER OF OPPORTUNITY

This dynamic concept of enterprise, helped not a little by the grim choice of making a go of it or perishing in the new land, saved many an immigrant from falling back to the status of people dependent for their livelihood upon the employment by others. Economic independence and self-determination marked a substantial part of the middle class.

The history of America exemplifies, as that of few other countries, the role of the middle class as developers and refiners of opportunity. Especially in the early days, its members took seeds of invention from other countries to plant in American soil. (In the twentieth century, the process was reversed.) They took the land and developed communities. They bought more land and developed cities. They added still more land and made the cities into metropolitan centers of increasing refinement. They invested in canals and railroads, highways and airlines, radio and television, building a huge network of transportation and communication.

They sponsored adventure and inquiry on the grand scale and added new dimensions to the American enterprise. They backed scientific inquiry and its technological application, thus aiding in the writing of a gigantic era in American history. In brief, they wove an ever more complex pattern of production, consumption, and service across the land, indeed, across the globe, refining styles, tastes, and modes of living in the process. If the basic conditions for new opportunity were created through the growth of population, if the basic design was created by the genius of leaders, its vast, long-range development and its constant improvement and refinement were carried forward by the middle class.

As different as the history of the middle class in America is from that in Europe, it should be noted that in basic principles it differs very little. Three examples may be cited: the development of opportunity; the attitude toward religion; and the process of decay.

DEVELOPMENT OF OPPORTUNITY

Members of the American middle class fought as stubbornly as their European counterparts whenever property, opportunity, and personal liberty were threatened. Regardless of which side they were on, they fought with conviction, courage, and determination. The issue may have been taxation without representation or emancipation of the slaves. It may have been freedom of speech, right of self-determination, civil rights or states' rights—the basic attitude of the members of the American middle class in facing and dealing with these and other issues was hardly different from that of their European peers.

However, the history of the American middle class is far more dynamic; it changes more abruptly, develops more rapidly, contains more crises and perhaps more achievements. In general, members of the middle class in America have shown themselves less conservative than those in Europe. Opportunities in America were larger and more original. Often, they came with a rush, as in the case of railroads, oil, and automobiles—and in overwhelming doses. Not infrequently, they put members of the middle class before a grim choice: take the risk or lose the chance! This choice made for dynamic action of high order and potency. If the American middle class showed itself to be less conservative, it was perhaps because it had precious little to hang on to. Much of what it brought about was fresh, new, and original.

133

The difference between the European and American middle classes was not based so much on the respective characters of the two groups as it was on the level of economic opportunity available to each. The essential difference was one of time. In America, the middle class succeeded rapidly because economic opportunity was ready for the picking. In past centuries, states and nations took a long time to develop conditions conducive to the growth of a middle class. Greece and Rome required hundreds of years to establish such conditions. In what today is called Germany, it took more than a thousand years to develop the kind of opportunity that could promote and sustain a middle class. Neither the Dark Ages nor the Age of Feudalism were conducive to the existence of a solid middle class because economic and political opportunities were suppressed rather than encouraged. As the time differential between the development of a middle class in Europe and America narrows down, the afore-mentioned differences are likely to diminish—and eventually disappear.

RELIGION—POLITICS

Another area in which no basic differences are revealed between the character of the American and the European middle class is in their respective attitudes toward religious authority and, (bearing in mind the European conflicts involving religion and politics) one may add, toward politics. I previously stated that the history of the middle class is an odd mixture of tough opposition and ready compromise. The statement applies to the history of the American middle class. Although the early settlers had just escaped from religious oppression and severe restriction by the authorities in European countries, they nevertheless showed the same tough and unrelenting attitude toward more liberal religious practices.

> Many religious restrictions existed in colonial days. The early settlers of Virginia were members of the Church of England and it was the practices of their church which were to be observed in the colony. In Massachusetts, for a long time every voter had to

be a member of a Congregational church. Strenuous efforts were made to bar immigrants belonging to other religious denominations. Dissenters and critics who appeared among the Puritans were frowned upon and sometimes severely punished, executed, or exiled into the wilderness. [5]

But as in Europe, where the attitude of the middle class eventually became amenable to compromise, so in America, during a much shorter period, the rigid attitude of intolerance and hostility gave way to one of relaxation and tolerance.

In the course of time, religious restrictions slowly relaxed. In law or practice or both, a broad religious liberty was gradually accorded to the people throughout the colonies. But it was not universal religious freedom. After the break with Great Britain, the first state constitutions, with some exceptions, excluded Catholics, Unitarians, Deists, and Jews from the right to vote and hold office in the new state governments. . . . The Old World heritage of religious intolerance and persecution had been severely shattered everywhere in America, even in the nine colonies with established churches, but many vestiges of religious discrimination remained to be cleared away. [6]

135

The American middle class has as fine a record of fighting for universal human rights and for freedom and equality, as any class, and possibly a superior record. The fight for political rights and for tolerance and individual liberty was eventually expressed in the doctrine of the inalienable rights of every man, woman, and child throughout the world, and thus became a hope and a message for the whole of mankind. This new voice of freedom, which was actually the rebirth of the ancient Roman *humanitas*, strongly influenced the early phase of the French Revolution.

From its very beginning, the middle class insisted that education accept a strong commitment to the idea of mankind. Horace Mann represents this commitment most clearly. His firm belief in human and natural rights led to a wide variety of humanitarian activities. Organized Christianity held strongly to this idea. In 1830, William Ellery Channing wrote: "We love our country much, but mankind more. . . . In all nations we recognize one great family."

Many humanitarian reforms are further evidence of the powerful influence of the middle class: abolition of slavery, poverty relief, prison reform, temperance, pacifism, women's rights, workers' rights, free education for the masses, wars against foreign aggression, the struggle for the United Nations, and many other progressive, enlightened, and liberal movements.

DECLINE

The earlier generalizations regarding other classes are equally valid for the American middle class. A hundred years ago, that class was guided largely by the seemingly unlimited dimensions of opportunity. Today, the emphasis is upon security and protection. Many of its members would rather have a well-paying job than be on their own, rather make use of other people's ideas than create their own, rather look to government to guarantee subsidies (in farming or in shipping), pensions (in jobs), protection (in sickness), deposits (in banks), than to pay for these and other services out of private resources. This development, necessary though it may be, affects the freedom and self-reliance of the individual person, thus contributing to the decline of the American middle class.

THE MIDDLE
CLASS—PRINCIPLES
OF FUNCTION

Filling the gap between the people and the leadership class, the middle class obviously has a close relationship to both. How this relationship is affected by the development and operation of the middle class, especially insofar as the interests of the people are concerned, is the subject of this chapter. We will also examine the role of the middle class in making possible a societal system that not only functions but grows and expands.

The middle class itself is not overly dynamic. It develops and refines opportunity in an orderly, methodical, profitable fashion. Yet, placed as it is between two dynamic groups—the people and the leadership class (one by reason of population growth, the other by reason of vision and ambition)—it can hardly help being affected by any change in their fortunes. Acting as a kind of liaison between the two groups, the middle class must be responsive to their fluctuations. How does this liaison operate in the function of the middle class?

Perhaps the most important effect results from the turn-over in the people's group and, to a lesser extent, in that of the leadership class. A constant exchange is going on between the three groups, with the middle class serving as a sort of clearing house. Briefly, those who succeed in advancing from the economic subsistence level join the middle class. Those who succeed in reaching the rarefied atmosphere of the leadership class are mostly graduates from the middle class. In reverse, those who fail to make the grade in the leadership class are apt to swell the ranks of the middle class. Finally those who fail as members of the middle class take their place with the people. This is an over-simplification, but basically a true description of the process.

Pitirim Sorokin shows the evolution of a middle class in the German city of Karlsruhe. When the first rural immigrants settled, 82 per cent were in the lower classes, 14 per cent in the middle classes, the remaining 4 per cent in the professional, i.e., educated class. Their sons advanced to the extent that 49 per cent belonged to the middle classes, 10 per cent to the advanced class, with 41 per cent remaining in the lower classes. Their grandsons made no progress in moving out of the lower classes, but 25 per cent of them were in the educated class, only 35 per cent in the middle classes, with 40 per cent still in the lower classes.[1] The gradual advancement was made possible by the economic opportunity developing in the established nation.

The middle class also functions as an institute, preparing and training potential leaders. This institute consists of three schools: that of the unbridled intellect marking future leaders, at first in revolution, later in establishing new leadership; the second school is of the carefully nourished intellect marking future leaders in science; the third school is a variation of the second marking future leaders in the arts.

138

SCHOOL FOR INTELLECT

All three schools stress intellect, since keen intelligence, a sharp analytical mind, and clear vision are needed to plan the exploitation of new opportunity accurately and efficiently. Again, a high degree of concentration and persistence is required to replace vested interests.

In the development of the three types of leadership, the middle class has virtually a monopoly, since neither the leadership class nor the people offer much in the way of training opportunities. Whenever history tells of the inauguration of a new era of economic opportunity in an established city, state, or nation, it speaks of the middle class. Chapter Six mentions outstanding leaders of the English, American, French, and Russian revolutions, showing that nearly all of them came from the middle class. Even those who originally had come from the ranks of the people had risen, by virtue of personality or intellectual ability, to middle-class status by the time the revolution broke out. However, most of these leaders were born of middle-class families, received an education, inherited intellectual qualities, and grew up in a stimulating environment.

The middle class harbors a larger number of intellectuals than the other classes. Often, it is the intellectuals rather than the people who suffer most harshly from the sterile inadequacy of an aging leadership class. It is they who react most strongly to the emptiness of the social activities and the futility of the economic climate. It is they who feel humiliated by the arrogance and abuse of power on the part of the leadership class. It is they who are outspoken in their condemnation of the prevailing regime, and eloquent in describing a vision of the future.

The scholars and thinkers, prophets and orators in ancient Israel, Egypt, Greece, Rome, as those in modern England, America, France, Russia, play nearly identical roles. They form the vanguard of leadership for those whom opportunity was denied. The natural opposition to the stale mentality of the expiring leadership class is the fiercely imaginative mind of the rising intellectual of the middle class.

SCHOOL FOR SCIENCE

Although less spectacular, the role of the carefully guided, well-disciplined intellect is hardly less important than that of the unbridled intellect. The aspirants to leadership in the domain of science work more with the tools of rational knowledge than with those of imagination and intuitive speculation. They know rather than guess. They work quietly rather than demonstrate boisterously. They are instrumental not so much in establishing a new leadership class as in helping to create the conditions upon which that class expands and prospers.

It is easy to see why men of science should come from the middle class. The time and effort involved in obtaining an education and in gaining the necessary experience require an expenditure of money which usually only the better-situated or middle-class family can afford. As was pointed out before, moderate or better-than-moderate circumstances are a common feature in the lives of noted scientists.

These carefully trained persons sometimes become central figures in planning and even in directing the course of the new leadership class. Neither the people nor members of the old leadership class are capable of exerting a similar influence; nor are other members of the middle class; nor are future leaders of the unbridled intellect. Some of the latter may have the ability to develop formulas for the exploitation of new opportunity. Some may have the vision to discern it; others, the determination to bring it to fruition. But only the men of science—or rather those among them who have vision, determination, and abiding faith—can make the special contribution of the scientist as a great leader.

Many nations and all ages had science leadership classes, although they employed different tools. The Greeks, says Walther Rathenau, had a mystic but not a scholastic culture; they had science but not technique. The Jews had a scholastic but not a *Forschungs* (pure research) culture. The Romans had free thought as well as technique but not science. The Egyptians and Chinese had technique but neither free thought nor *Forschung* nor inner mysticism. [2]

In the contemporary world, men of science are working in teams along functional lines. In another age, the technically gifted furnished leadership. Looking back thirty and fifty years, we can see Edison, Ford, De Forest, Steinmetz, Taylor, Wright of architecture, the Wrights of aviation, and many others providing industrial leadership, thus putting upon their age the stamp of their genius. These men were of the middle class.

Van Loon points out the lack of appreciation of technical talent in our own age. In the United States, people have so many machines to do their bidding they no longer respect creative genius. The professionally trained army of engineers is so large that any kind of talent required can be obtained promptly. Intellectual resources are so rich that the movies attract little attention when they mention writers and other authors and artists, except in the case of an outstanding production. This situation, Van Loon believes, is an exact parallel to that of ancient Greece, where twelve million slaves served five million freemen. The Greeks had little respect for their artists. The names of the men who built the temples and stadia are mostly unknown to us.[3]

If our men of science are largely functionaries, it is because in our age science has become frozen in patterns of function. So sure has modern man become of the wonders of science that he has put it into harness: a novel version of Pegasus and the peasant. Where science used to be dreamed, it is now being retailed in the classroom. Once the vanguard of opportunity, it is now the tail of a procession. Science will be a phoenix again when new opportunities rise from the ashes of a moribund concept of security and protection. For only in the climate of great opportunities can science be free and can the scientifically gifted become great leaders.

SCHOOL FOR THE ARTS

The middle class's cultural contributions are probably as important as their economic ones, but they do not go hand in hand. History shows that a decline in the middle class's economic importance does not impair a city's or nation's cultural and artistic importance, rather it frequently marks the very highest development of culture and the arts. During the final stage of its history, Athens saw such great thinkers and artists as Pericles, Euripides, Sophocles, Thucydides, Aristophanes, Democritus, Socrates, Plato, Aristotle, Isocrates, Apelles, Praxiteles, and Lysippus.

The arts also flowered amid the cracks which signaled the beginning of the decline of ancient Rome, where a coldly practical orientation hardly encouraged great art. Rome never had greater poets, orators, historians, architects, artists, and philosophers than during the reign of the Caesars when murder, intrigue, corruption, and waste on a large scale accompanied the break-up of the empire. A decadent century was brightly illuminated by Lucretius, Cicero, Virgil, Horace, Livy, and, later, by Seneca, Plutarch, and Tacitus. Nor should one forget those responsible for the decorative use of arch and column in the triumphal monuments of the Caesars, the baths of Caracalla and Diocletian, or the magnificent basilicas built in Rome and many other cities.

The thirteenth and fourteenth centuries were marked by the success of the middle class in Venice. This era saw great cultural achievements in arts and letters. But when the world came to recognize Italy as the leader of European civilization, the economic power of the middle class in Venice and Florence had passed its peak. At a time when mercantilism had grown old, the declining years of Venice were brilliantly brightened by the genius of her artists. Titian, Tintoretto, Paolo Veronese, Palladio, Giorgione, and Sansovino lived and worked after the disastrous wars of the League of Cambrai.

Centuries later, when the cathedrals of Amiens, Poitiers, and Chartres represented the artistic peak in medieval architecture, the economic power of the middle class had been broken. As a civic building, the cathedral rose with the guilds. As a masterpiece, it emerged when the guilds had passed their peak.

In a similar way, the cultural acme of the Netherlands was reached in the seventeenth century, which although it was marked by much turbulence and revolution, was also the age of Frans Hals, Rembrandt Van Rijn, and Van Dyck.

In seventeenth-century England, torn by civil war, the names of Shakespeare, Marlowe, Bacon, and Raleigh began to shine on the firmament of English art and culture.[4]

The great cultural and artistic era of seventeenth- and eighteenth-century France blossomed at a time when the power of the middle class had given way to a regime of absolute autocracy. Philosophers and writers like Descartes, Pascal, Abbé de Saint-Pierre, Turgot, Marquis de Condorcet, and Voltaire; and artists like Watteau, Chardin, Boucher, and Fragonard gave this era its cultural and artistic greatness.

Art in Germany was at its highest early in the nineteenth century, when Europe resounded to the blows inflicted by Napoleon's armies. It was the period of Goethe, Schiller, Beethoven, Schubert, Hegel, Schinkel, and other men of genius.

This evidence of the creation of great art (regardless of the reasons for its flowering) underlines another important function of the middle class: its contribution to the advance of civilization. By its ambition and industry, the middle class is an indispensable factor in the economic development of the nation, in the creation of wealth, and in the attainment of military strength and political power. But upon this same foundation of economic success, the middle class also contributes to the development of the arts and sciences, thus directly influencing the advance of civilization not only within the boundaries of its own political organization, but for all Mankind.

143

THE ARTS AND THE NATION

The arts require subsidy. Since the young nation is usually pressed with problems of survival, the people have neither time nor leisure for the arts. As the interests of artists are often alien to material values, and their work not too rewarding in the financial sense, artists must be supported. Putting it crudely, they must bide their time until the nation makes enough money to support them. More importantly, they must wait until the nation as a whole acquires a sense of artistic appreciation. The two conditions hang together, since without the latter the nation would not support the artist even if it were able to. The United States seems to be in this second phase. It has outstanding painters, sculptors, poets, and composers, but the people do not pay them the homage paid to Michelangelo, Rodin, Goethe, or Beethoven. When enough Americans have acquired the appreciation of great new art along with that of a great new car, and when they have the money for both, perhaps the American artist will find himself duly honored.

It is not enough for wealthy collectors to import paintings by Rubens and Rembrandt, Greek columns, Flemish silverware, Dutch porcelain, Spanish handwoven rugs, or a copy of the first printed edition of the Bible. It is not enough for a wealthy family to support a promising young artist. By taxing themselves either directly or through the government, the people themselves must foster the arts, build opera houses, subsidize symphony orchestras, organize art schools, and support cultural institutions. For this development to take place, artistic appreciation and financial generosity must exist on a large scale.

The arts must wait for the nation to attain a degree of wealth, a useful concept of leisure, and a belief in its world mission. However strongly the individual may feel about the arts, their advance in the interest of the group cannot be detached from economic reality. That realization is not born with the nation; it is born with the successful economic development of the nation, which is the task of the middle class. Conversely, artistic achievement does not die by reason of its own exhaustion. It dies because of the collapse of the nation's wealth and power. There is no reason why Greek art could not have gone on to still greater heights, still more perfect forms of expression, except for the decay of Greece itself. The same argument applies to other periods of great art—in Venice, Flanders, or seventeenth-century England.

At such times, the nation can no longer inspire the artist to greater effort because it is fighting for its life. No longer can the rich give generously because, having lost important sources of income, they are struggling to retain what is left of their wealth. The end of the artist comes slowly. For a while he continues on the momentum of his own creativeness. The pendulum of the artistic achievement keeps swinging back and forth. Eventually the artistic effort follows the decline of the nation's fortunes. Immediate passion freezes into remote tradition. The magnificence of the nation's art becomes grand history.

Through its economic success, the middle class makes possible the artistic achievement and the flowering of the arts. This development is not the result of deliberate design, let alone careful planning. It is brought about as a by-product of economic success, just as the development of new opportunity may be considered a by-product of a high birth rate. In these cases, neither the middle class nor the people are aware of the larger consequences of their action. In striving for financial gain, members of the middle class have neither time nor inclination to think of artistic achievement in national, let alone world, dimensions.

As the middle class does not deliberately create the arts in the nation, it can hardly claim credit for the contribution which the arts make either to the nation or to civilization. It is idle to speculate on the middle class as a powerful and independent force fighting to keep the arts great or even alive. High ideals, artistic devotion, and noble sacrifice are not among its principal ingredients.

MEANING

Placed between the set routine of the people and the dynamic effort of the leadership class, the middle class operates on a principle of practical utilization rather than a law of nature. It transforms the broad vision of the leadership class into solid realization. It guides the limited function of the people into the broad channels of useful enterprise. Where the people plow their unpretentious acres, the middle class builds roads to connect them. Where the former lives in scattered cabins, the latter promotes the growth of communities. Where the people exchange goods on a barter basis, the middle class coins money and promotes exchange on a commercial scale.

Where the people may do things with their muscles and mules, the middle class uses machines and tools. Where brawn reigns in one group, brains rule in the other. Where the people may settle for subsistence, the middle class demands the comforts of civilization. Where the people speak the idiom of functional activity, the middle class converses in the more refined language of individual enterprise. Where the former are satisfied with unexciting labor and reward, the latter seeks achievement and acclaim. In these and similar terms, the middle class is the creator and standard-bearer of civilization.

In the pursuit of its aspirations, the middle class is instrumental in developing and expanding work opportunity for the people. Roads, farms, communities, and machines are meaningless without people traveling, cultivating, populating, and operating them. This relationship is a two-way street. The middle class needs the people as much as the people need the middle class. However, the initiative must come from the middle class. If there were no middle class, opportunity for advancement would be denied to most people, as it was in pre-industrial societies when the middle class was generally small or non-existent. In our age, widespread poverty, ignorance, and misery indicate those areas where a substantial middle class does not exist, as in many of the developing countries of Asia, Africa, and Latin America.

If in dynamic character the middle class stands apart from both the people and the leadership class, in practical importance it matches either. The nation could not function effectively without it nor can wealth be created in large measure. The leadership class would lack the means by which to control relations with the people, while the people would lack the channels through which all of them can, in theory, and some do, in reality, advance their fortunes.

Because the leadership class keeps creating new opportunity, and because it is not the function of the people to take a direct part in the creative process, the role of the middle class in simplifying, broadening, and thus enlarging opportunity is of vital importance. Its historical role has been no less than to develop civilization. Cities could not be built in methodical fashion nor invention be stimulated into tangible achievement without the middle class. Science would be without long-term opportunity, and the arts would never prosper. Civilization might never have become the magnificent creation that it is, and the aspirations of the many would never have been realized. Refinement would be unknown, and beauty wither into a lone straggler. If the people and the leadership class serve as dynamic elements—the former in unwittingly creating opportunity, the latter in knowingly organizing its exploitation—the middle class is the instrument through which these values are given tangible expression.

Again, the middle class is the weak link in the human society. Ambitious and enterprising though it is, the middle class lacks creative ability. For sustained activity, such as the function of industry and commerce, the support of education and the arts, or the preservation of traditions and credos, its ingenuity is adequate. But for the larger tasks of creative enterprise, such as the founding of cities, the opening up of channels of communication, the pioneering of discovery, the design of new industries, or the development of original ideas into forces of major importance, it must wait for the leadership class to show the way. Before the middle class can help enlarge economic opportunity, it must wait for leaders among the inventors, speculators, planners, engineers, financiers, builders, statesmen, and others to call it into being. Before it can build systems of roads, streets, and bridges, it must wait for the pioneers, in and out of government, to underwrite the risk and face the losses. Before it could go west, it had to wait for leaders among the missionaries, adventurers, trappers, scouts, and prospectors to show the way to the furs, skins, gold, silver, copper, and oil.

The middle class can be as strong and successful as economic opportunity will permit. But the irony of the middle class is that, in the modern world and perhaps to a lesser degree in previous ages, the opportunity permitted far more than the middle class ever realized. Due to its great contribution to civilization and culture, which was not confined to one nation, and due to its important role in commerce and industry, which involved many nations, the middle class had the unique opportunity, economic and otherwise, to be a powerful instrumentality for the promotion of understanding, cooperation, and peace among Mankind. However,

147

to be able to exploit that opportunity, it would have had to display qualities of leadership, opposing in the process leadership classes of nations throughout the world. Obviously, requirements of such global dimension are beyond either the character or the capability of the middle class.

It is unwise to expect the middle class to fight the evils of nationalism. It is futile to expect from it great ideals or the devotion and sacrifice that go with them. The nation is to the middle class what the mother is to the child. To the nation it owes birth, growth, and success. Called into being by the nation, the middle class is dependent upon it for economic opportunity and its resulting gains. The middle class is well aware of this dependence. With good reason does it act as the staunch supporter of national and sometimes nationalistic aspirations. The evils of the nation, of which war is the greatest, are fully shared by the middle class.

In search of profitable venture, the middle class becomes the willing agent of the interests and ambitions as interpreted by the nation's leadership class. The middle class is patient enough to work hard for the exploitation of economic opportunity as it develops within and without the nation, but it is not unselfish enough to help realize the great ideals of civilization. It is courageous enough to stand up to the leadership class where its own interests—economic opportunity, the rights of property, personal liberty—are concerned. But it is neither enlightened enough nor bold enough to fight for the advancement, let alone the liberation, of Mankind.

The failure of the middle class to transcend the limitations of the nation, to use its outstanding abilities and vast resources for the utilization of unrivaled opportunities toward the creation of a supernational civilization, is perhaps the greatest shortcoming of the middle class.

As the middle class has never played a greater role than that of an important development and refinement unit in the nation's framework, apparently it is not meant for a higher function, at least not under existing societal principles. Is the future likely to change the basic principles by which the middle class operates?

WILL TECHNOLOGY MAKE
A DIFFERENCE?

If technology continues to advance, it may serve to promote industrial development in the poorer countries, to further refine industrial productivity in the more affluent countries, and to exert a powerful effect upon the economies of the remaining countries. Whatever its effect, it may have a similar impact upon middle classes around the globe. The middle classes may be the instrument through which the process of development and refinement will take place, creating better living conditions for the majority of the world's population.

Will the economic advance of the people adversely affect the middle classes or population increase or efforts to abolish war or greater international cooperation? I do not think so; on the contrary, each of these developments is likely to intensify, enrich, and enlarge economic and related opportunities, thus creating for middle class members ever new and larger areas in which to apply their industry, ability, ambition, and intelligence.

WILL GREATER GOVERNMENT POWER
MAKE A DIFFERENCE?

As history indicates, the middle class may be expected to oppose stubbornly greater government power and control if its members feel they interfere with what they consider their rightful interests and opportunities. Again, they may readily cooperate with that greater power if they expect substantial gain. Under a dictatorial regime, the middle class may temporarily lose some of its privileges, as it has lost them time and again in the past; but even then it managed simply to change its dress from that of an economic to that of a political middle class. Speaking of the communist revolution in modern China, H. G. Creel says:

Certain traditional attitudes have been in the Communists' favor. George E. Taylor goes so far as to say that the Chinese Communists "stem from the traditional Chinese bureaucratic ruling class," and that the Chinese Communist party represents "the bureaucracy, with all its tradition of political, social and economic monopoly." [5]

As the totalitarian design gradually mellows into quasi-democratic shape, as it usually does with the passage of time, the middle-class bureaucracy finds little hardship and no hesitation in changing back promptly to the traditional middle-class role. Such is the extent of its adaptability and versatility. In the case of fascist regimes, it was even saved this metamorphosis, maintaining its far-flung operations right through the respective ages of terror.

The function of the middle class is so deeply ingrained in the societal system that no future development is likely to change the principles by which it operates. It has lived through revolutions before without changing any of its basic principles, and no doubt will do so again. The institution of the middle class is probably as secure as that of the people or the leadership class. Unlike the people, it depends upon no one for its livelihood; and unlike the leadership class, it does not have to create new opportunity.

Whatever the future, members of middle classes the world over may be expected to stand ready and eager to play their part, to accept calculated risks as well as planned rewards to increase if possible tangible assets, but at least to maintain power, prestige and influence.

CHAPTER
ELEVEN

LESSONS
OF
THE
PAST

After more than five thousand years of societal history, the people are still the unwitting creators of new opportunity, the leadership class still the exploiters, and the middle class still the developers and refiners. If the people are to attain dignity of life, they will have to attain it through other than the traditional pattern of societal relationships. Can the future bring about the profound changes called for in the basic reconstruction of society? Can man learn the lessons of the past?

FACTORS RESPONSIBLE FOR
THE PLIGHT OF THE PEOPLE

It has been stressed that the people's basic problem is their dependence on others. The pressure of physical needs, the fear of their masters, and the desire for protection create conditions of servitude for the people. However, in the fixed relationship between the people and the leadership class, neither is more important than the other; they are indispensable to each other's existence and function.

Dependence in itself is neither bad nor even avoidable. Where it does become bad, and perhaps avoidable, is where it is exploited to the point of abuse. Excessive exploitation was a major reason why the people followed the leadership of Tiberius Gracchus, Spartacus, Jesus, Wat Tyler, Martin Luther, and Karl Marx. If, under existing societal conditions, exploitation is necessary, must it be applied to the point of abuse?

While the leadership class must depend upon the people for the purpose of exploiting opportunity (see Chapter Four), it does not generally exploit the people for the sake of exploitation. It would be more accurate to say that its use of the people is determined by the conditions of opportunity. The opportunity to develop new land places hardships upon the people, as in the case of modern Israel. The opportunity to gain world leadership involves sacrifices by the people, as in the case of the Soviet Union. The opportunity to develop successful enterprise in the clothing industry may create the sweatshop, as it did in the United States early in the twentieth century. The opportunity for a poorly mechanized industry (employing mostly home labor) to compete with a highly mechanized industry may compel a low wage level. Or simply the opportunity to maintain conditions, in which the people remain poor and ignorant, may explain exploitation that is continued over a long period of time, as in the case of feudal systems in Arab countries.

This is not to say that there may not be other ways in which the relationship between the people and the leadership class can and does function. The determining factor in the exploitation of the people may not lie primarily either with the people or the leadership class but may be found in opportunity itself. In order to correct the abuses of exploitation, one may have to deal with opportunity as the responsible factor. Since the leadership class is the one that controls existing opportunity and strives to exploit future opportunity, it is obviously through that class that one must consider the element of opportunity.

But as soon as one inquires into ways of controlling new opportunity, one runs into problems of motivation. Leaders exploit opportunity to affirm their identity or, more precisely, the characteristics that set them apart from other leaders. This identity is indispensable to a meaningful existence for either the individual or the group. The exploitation of opportunity is, therefore, an essential tool in the realization of a leader's aspirations.

If opportunity can be controlled at all, it must not be at the expense of identity. To a certain extent, the exploitation of opportunity, urged by the need for identity, is necessary and unavoidable. The question is: to what extent? A possible answer is: the extent beyond which exploitation becomes excessive and, therefore, abusive. A few examples may illustrate the point.

In a sense, labor is opposed to management because their basic objectives are different. The announced prime objective of labor is the welfare of the worker; that of management, the realization of a profit. If labor were to call a general strike in pursuit of its objective, it might be accused of excessive exploitation of its opportunity inasmuch as it would be placing its own interests above those of the commonweal. The poor are opposed to the rich. The basic interest of the one is to obtain the necessities of life; of the other, to keep and if possible to add to his wealth. If the poor person threatened the rich person in pursuit of his objective, he might be accused of excessive exploitation. The democratic nation opposes the communist nation; its basic philosophy disagrees with that of communism. If this disagreement caused one nation to go to war with the other, this might be considered an excessive exploitation of opportunity.

The need is to restrain the identity (that is, the aspirations) of leadership. This need is not likely to be met through voluntary concessions by nations nor by the free determination of their leadership groups. They would thereby jeopardize the very principles upon which not only their success but their survival is predicated. By making basic or major concessions to, say, communism, the United States would probably weaken not only its democratic principles and tradition but its world leadership, form of government, and way of life, not to mention the spiritual values contained in all of them. The same could be said of the Soviet Union were it to make basic or major concessions to the United States and its democratic principles.

Nor can this need (to restrain the excessive aspirations of leadership identity) be met merely by enlarging the size of the respective units, as in the organization of the North Atlantic bloc, the Soviet bloc, or the neutral bloc. The process of enlargement may or may not be a preliminary step leading to the eventual establishment of a world authority. By itself, however, enlargement would not produce new principles of cooperation among the opposing units or bring about basic changes in the relations between the people and leadership groups.

The aspirations of leadership may attain a broader sweep, but their power would be likely to remain as autonomous and their opposition to the establishment of a world authority as determined as ever. Exploitation would take place on a larger scale. If before people were exploited on the regional or national level, now they would be exploited on the continental level. If before people were expected to die, if necessary, for the feudal lord, the king, or the fatherland, now they would be expected to give their lives for the North Atlantic Alliance or the World Soviet Alliance.

VIEWS OF SOCIAL THINKERS

In order to give realistic consideration to ways of attaining the dignity of life for people everywhere, it is necessary to consider not only the complex pattern of leadership identity but the whole of human society. If the interpretation of human society's past performance presented in this book is valid, then it is evident that the improvement of society and, with it, the establishment of better conditions for the people cannot depend upon the expansion of man's social nature, as suggested by Aristotle and Aquinas. While that expansion has promoted cooperation on a large scale in virtually all areas of the human endeavor (political, institutional, scientific, technical, professional, industrial; artistic, inspirational, spiritual; educational, philosophical, religious, etc.), it also has had the effect of enlarging and intensifying opposition in substantial degree. If past is prelude, then it is doubtful that the future expansion of man's social nature will improve the societal system.

Nor is it likely that fear and distrust form the basic element of society, as argued by Machiavelli and Hobbes. While it is true that fear and distrust are not only deeply ingrained in human nature but are fostered by deliberate design to gain or to maintain leadership support, it is no less true that cooperation and trust are important elements in society. Even though cooperation may originate in fear and distrust of a third party, it is still true that in order to make cooperation effective, an element of faith and confidence is required. If the fear of God causes a person to join a church, his faith in religion is still the guiding light and motivation. If fear and distrust of the Soviet Union cause some nations to create a defensive alliance, it is still true that their cooperation is not likely to work effectively without some degree of faith in each other.

Because these and similar views are partly true and partly not, it is doubtful whether they can serve as a realistic premise upon which to evaluate various means of improving human society. Taken by themselves, the reorganization of government as proposed by Henri de Saint-Simon and Auguste Comte; the policy of laissez-faire as stated by Herbert Spencer and William Sumner; the theory of private property as propounded by John Locke and Lewis Henry Morgan; and the revolutionary program of Karl Marx cannot be considered a hopeful approach because none deals primarily with the basic problem which is the "Mankind problem," as evidenced by the gross inadequacy of the existing societal relationship. It is not that these and other social thinkers go wrong or too far. On the contrary, they do not go far enough. None considers the people's dynamic (if unwitting) function as creators of opportunity or its counterpart—their economic insecurity and political dependence. None seems to consider the leadership class as tied to an indispensable pattern of identity and distinction, balanced by its authority over and control of the people, enacting a law of nature. Hence, the approach underlying these views deals with some of the parts. Not one appears to deal with the whole of which all are a part, namely Mankind.

The segmented character of these views is matched by the segmented development of the human society. The oppositional, often hostile character of the various groups and their leadership must account in large measure for the stagnation of what is here considered true progress, that is, progress for Mankind as a whole. A better society, uniting the great majority in peaceful striving, is not likely to be attained unless the existing pattern of leadership identity is altered, unless the very fundamental principles of the societal system are rethought, redesigned, and reorganized.

---

156   PROGRESS FOR MANKIND

The implication that Mankind as a whole has made no real progress through the ages will be challenged. Spencer, Comte, Turgot, and many others have maintained that the human society has made very real progress. Language, for example, has markedly benefited all of Mankind. Brutal force has given way to civilized procedure in much of the modern world. The moral awareness of right and wrong marks much of man's social behavior. Increasing communication amoug the peoples of the world, growing understanding of different religions, and mounting exchange of ideas in numerous international conferences are helping to create a common conception of minimum requirements for a better society. In brief, improved education and broader knowledge have resulted in expanding and refining culture and civilization throughout the world.

In such terms as expanding production and distribution on all levels of society or increasing opportunity for the individual person to develop his own genius, there has also been considerable progress in the last three or four centuries. Before the First World War, most people in the United States were apparently convinced of the inevitability of this type of progress. At the same time, there has been a pronounced trend toward ever higher standards of living, increased life expectancy, and expanded opportunity for the individual person not only in the United States but also in other parts of the world, notwithstanding setbacks due to wars and revolutions. Is it then not obvious that society is making continued progress?

Doubts may be raised as to whether the progress has benefited all of mankind. Language not only facilitates understanding, it complicates communication; it has been quite effective in separating, even antagonizing, rather than uniting, people. If brutal force has given way to just and orderly procedure, if moral awareness of right and wrong marks much of man's social behavior, if knowledge has resulted in expanding and refining culture and civilization—why does the greater part of humanity continue to be beset by poverty, misery, slavery, exploitation, group dominance, loss of individual values, and, above all, war, in a seemingly ever rising degree of intensity? If there is a net gain for Mankind in growing understanding, welfare, cooperation, and security, why have basic faults in the societal relationship not been corrected, especially those that are reflected in the limitation or the absence of freedom, security, and dignity for the people everywhere? Again, if there has been no net gain in these and related matters for Mankind in the past, why should such gains be expected in the future?

Progress for Mankind cannot be measured by progress or the lack of it in different countries. It must be evaluated in terms of the overall development of human society. If a developing country in Asia, Africa, or Latin America is enabled through the application of modern methods of production and distribution to record substantial economic progress, but uses it in an attempt to make gains by armed force, then there is no gain for Mankind. If the United States uses some of the means that created the highest material standard of living ever for the purpose of creating the hydrogen bomb, then there is no gain for Mankind.

Technological and scientific advance so far has not brought real progress to Mankind. To be sure, the advances made possible by Edison, Ford, and others are substantial. But if the focus is widened beyond technical significance, material advances are severely qualified by social problems. Automation, speed-up, loss of human values, insecurity, and unemployment are results contrary to the idea of progress.

In the United States, there has been much progress. But if the scene were broadened to encompass all Mankind, the American standard of living would lose much of its proud and progressive meaning when compared with the standards of two billion people of different races, colors, and nationality. And if time were stretched to a point where it covered all of Mankind's history, one would be hard put to find any evidence of gains used for the benefit of people everywhere.

On past experience, there is considerable reason to doubt man's ability to solve problems created by the advance of science and technology. The uses made of new ideas and devices are such that they cancel out the very improvements they make possible. The machine is a vast improvement over slave labor, but it has not brought individual freedom; it has been used to exploit man. Radar and jet planes, corporate management and computer systems, atomic fission and opinion control indicate how greatly techniques can be improved. But their application also shows how firmly man is chained to the principle of gain at the expense of others.

In solving one major problem, man creates or intensifies another, thus making it impossible to find a lasting solution to any problem. Gutenberg's invention made possible printing from movable type but created the problem of mass distortion and abuse. The metropolis solved the problem of greater opportunity for the individual but created that of economic insecurity for large masses of people concentrated in small areas. Medical science solved in part the problem of premature death but created that of overpopulation.

In our own age, the machine solved the problem of low wages but discouraged craftsmanship and created the problem of dependence upon production schedules. Labor unions helped solve or at least alleviate this particular difficulty but intensified the problem of rising labor costs. Mass production

158

solved the problem of rising labor costs but created that of large-scale depressions. Greater federal authority and control seemed to provide the answer to the problem of major depressions but created that of authoritarianism, which in turn threatens to weaken individual identity. Thus the chain reaction works out to the disadvantage of Mankind.[1]

As was pointed out previously, technology (if it continues to advance) is not likely to change the traditional relationship between leadership class and the people. On the contrary, it may make for greater centralization of authority, for stricter group control, and therefore for further depreciation of the importance of the individual person and further loosening of family ties. More than ever, the "public people" will prevail over the "private people."[2]

Nor is the advance of technology likely to create a group which can speak for Mankind. Cooperation among nations may expand, but only to the extent that it will serve the interests of the participating nations as against the interests of other nations or groups of nations. Given the existing pattern of the societal structure, the application of techno- 159 logical improvements will probably cause the emergence of more powerful factions and of more tragic conflicts between them. Far from bringing the unity of Mankind closer, it is likely to inflict graver wounds upon Mankind than ever were inflicted before.

While the advance of technology has helped man to see the world increasingly as a whole, it has also helped create or strengthen barriers rather than remove them. It has broadened and deepened the use of partisan concepts; it has intensified rivalry, conflict, and war; it has enlarged the size, power, and influence of groups and their leadership. Above all, the technological superiority of the West has "subjugated the world and held it in political or economic bondage until very recent times; it is still disposing of the destinies and fates of many non-Western peoples. It is perhaps a primary factor in the disunity of Mankind."[3]

These negative results should not be blamed on the advance of technology but on the failure of man. He permitted technology to dominate the development of societal relationships toward greater partisanship where conceivably he might have used technology to change partisan concepts and bring about broader understanding of societal relationships.

TRUE PROGRESS IS FOR THE PEOPLE

True progress should be measured in terms of the people rather than the leadership group or the middle class. While the organized function of society would not be possible without leaders, Mankind would survive because its raw material, the people, would continue to exist and to multiply; in time, new leaders would arise. Again, civilization and cultural achievements would decay if the middle class were eliminated, but the people would carry on the basic processes of humanity; in time, a new middle class would emerge. But Mankind would be unthinkable without the people, as the earth would be unthinkable without the soil which produces the rich varieties of nature.

By the same token, the achievements of the leadership group and the middle class cannot generally be considered progress for Mankind. For what is the greatness of a nation if it is bought at the price of countless human lives lost in war? Nor can "freedom" be called true progress if it is maintained by the enslavement and servitude of great numbers of people. Even the advances of education, science, technology, and other disciplines cannot be rated basic progress within the broad framework of Mankind if the use of their achievements causes the increased dependence of and decreased freedom for the individual person.

Nothing is likely to affect the welfare of Mankind more profoundly or more lastingly than what is or is not done for all of the people. The historical record shows that man has endeavored many times but has rarely succeeded in doing anything for the benefit of all of the people, and thus for the benefit of Mankind. This is perhaps as it should be. The principle of individuality argues against universal control in all affairs at all times. If every individual act conformed to universal criteria, no opportunity would be left for individual choice and motivation. It follows that a consideration of the interest of Mankind should be applied principally to issues and problems of major importance.

Leadership classes have not used the people as the basic material of which Mankind is made and which quite naturally binds it together. They have used them as the basic material of which nations, religions, races, industries, labor unions, political parties, and other factions are made. They have used them in the service of each and, at the same time, against the interests of each. In the process, the common and natural ties binding the people together have been smashed into a million fragments and have divided Mankind into innumerable diverse and often opposing units.

Notwithstanding many noble attempts through the ages, man has never solved the dilemma of the people because he has never approached the problem in terms of Mankind. If the people are to be helped in basic ways and in a lasting manner, they must be helped as members of Mankind first —regardless of land, climate, education, religion, racial, political, economic, or social status.

161

In this sense, the people and Mankind are synonymous.

CHAPTER TWELVE

THE
LEADERSHIP
OF
MANKIND

MANKIND FRAMEWORK
THE ONLY SOLUTION

The foregoing chapters suggest that if the people are to attain freedom from the traditional burden of insecurity, dependence, and exploitation, they can do so only as equals in a broader societal framework than the one existing today. The broader framework can be no less than the whole of Mankind. This is the conclusion of the book.

Of the countless efforts on behalf of the people in the past, none has brought them individual freedom, economic security, and personal dignity. In the West, these efforts dealt only with partial dimensions and segmented perspectives, not with the entire scope of the dimensions and perspectives of Mankind. In the East, they dealt with the greater-than-Mankind dimensions of the Universe, by-passing the dimensions and perspectives of existing Mankind. The "Mankind perspective," which signifies freedom for all, avoids both these pitfalls. Because it represents the middle road, it is the one perspective that promises success.

The "Mankind framework" is the only one that satisfies the moral as well as the practical requisites of freedom and dignity for all people regardless of social standing, economic level, religious belief, or political allegiance. It is morally wrong that the material success of the minority should depend upon the physical exploitation of the majority; that, as a result of this exploitation, the majority should be deprived of the full development of its potential; that the principles of human dignity, equality, freedom, and justice should be frequently disregarded, abused, or distorted under the existing societal system.

As forced dependence and ruthless exploitation, in whatever name, are morally wrong, so the attainment of the aforementioned principles for all people everywhere is morally right. It would appear that the only way to replace the system of exploitation with a system benefiting all is to transfer the societal order, of which the people are an intrinsic part, from the controlling interest of the segments (management and labor; science and technology; community and nation; law and government; institution and discipline; race and religion; art and philosophy; culture and civilization) to the controlling interest of the whole: Mankind.

It is doubtful how much longer technological advance will permit the people to be used as an instrument of exploitation. Some experts believe that continued advance may cause unemployment on a scale never before experienced. Unemployment, in turn, will stimulate new ideas in the use of leisure. Experimentation will take place on many fronts. Intermediate phases will mark the gradual progression, it is hoped, from a condition of insecurity, dependence and exploitation for many to the eventual attainment of a state of freedom, independence, and dignity for all.

August Heckscher has given a description of some of the intermediate phases: In a society such as the United States, which is highly urbanized and becoming more so, unemployment, the central dilemma of advancing technology, sets the pattern. The people enter the labor force later and retire earlier. Shorter working days and shortened work weeks will make for ever more leisure, and for ever more aimless people. Education not for eight or ten or twelve years but for a person's entire life will have to provide the answer. Education will cultivate greater interest in the arts, develop special skills in diverse hobbies and crafts, and above all, arouse people's interest in more humane pursuits such as building better cities, providing more recreation, devising more meaningful outlets for surplus energy, and creating more attractive landscapes.[1]

All this, however, may be no more than an empty if lovely vision unless the entire effort is rooted in the soil of Mankind—not by the people of one nation but by the people of all nations. The vision can hardly become reality in a world torn by rampant nationalism and chauvinism, and bleeding under the whip of hatred, cruelty, narrow prejudice, and reckless violence.

PRESENT SOCIETAL SYSTEM
BEYOND REPAIR

There is well-nigh universal agreement that twentieth-century society is in a state of grave disrepair. In 1931, Carl Gustav Jung wrote: "Along the great highroads of the world, everything seems desolate and outworn. Seized by an exhausting anxiety, modern man has lost his sense of direction." Says Erich Kahler: "Everything is in flux, everything is open to question, everything is involved in perpetual change and dissolution." Since Oswald Spengler, many historians and philosophers have compared the crises now universal in Western civilization with the mental climate of Europe during the decline and fall of Rome and the waning of the Middle Ages. Says Warren Wagar: "Before this destiny the individual man stands somehow helpless ... The serious literature of most Western countries is now drenched with apocalyptic imagery. The 'cyclical' historians, Spengler, Toynbee, Sorokin and their disciples, predict the imminent going-under of modern civilization. A whole generation of men of faith, exponents of a neo-orthodox 'theology of crisis,' have rediscovered the doctrine of ineradicable original sin. The most characteristic new departure in Continental philosophy, existentialism, finds anxiety the normal condition of the self as it trembles precariously on the brink of death and meaninglessness."[2]

Since the prevailing societal system can neither solve nor even weather the problems threatening the contemporary age, it will become their victim. Poverty and racial strife, the rising flood of population, loss of identity, disappearance of values, tyranny of hunger and disease, nuclear war not between nations but between continents—these and many related problems are among the uncontrolled forces providing the bitter proof that the existing societal system is beyond repair.

The meaning of the high drama of our age—noted, examined, and analyzed in an endless sequence of books, articles, monographs, anthologies, lectures, speeches, and reports—may be summarized in a single sentence: *Absolute segmentation is no longer a viable principle in modern society.*

All past societies were characterized by principles of absolute segmentation. Modern society, expecially the nation, is marked by:

> its insistence (in a variety of leadership groups) upon absolute autonomy in the conduct of its affairs;
>
> its moral indifference and shallow conscience;
>
> its unwillingness to sacrifice any part of its identity (often held sacred and untouchable) for the benefit of all;
>
> its obstinate and unreasonable pride in clinging to traditions and rituals that have often become hollow and meaningless;
>
> its deep-seated, sometimes hot-tempered prejudice;
>
> its stiff, slow-moving, unenlightened bureaucracy;
>
> its lack of vision and imagination, coupled with jealous suspicion, even hatred of and discrimination against almost anything resembling original and creative thought.

These properties only too often characterize some of the controlling authorities of contemporary nations and races, management and labor, disciplines and institutions, cultures and civilizations.

The implication seems clear: the process of the dissolution of modern society underlines the urgent need to think in terms of the creation of a new societal system to replace the existing one. While this book is about the people, obviously it is idle to consider their liberation simply within the framework of the people. It must be considered within—and only within—the framework of Mankind.

The abrupt and radical change of the present societal system would probably jeopardize, perhaps even destroy the position, influence, and authority of prevailing powers. In contrast, a gradual and limited change in line with changing times would give them an opportunity to compromise with and adjust to threatening situations: demands for equality, advancing technology, greater leisure, and growing emphasis of the identity and dignity of the individual person. Would the cooperation of prevailing powers be a realistic expectation?

Judging from past history, it may be expected that prevailing powers, convinced of their rightful position, sold on their obvious importance, and lost in their own vanity, would be unable to grasp the need for basic changes, let alone to accept it. The sweeping concessions that the new leadership, . . . "Mankind leadership," must demand are not likely to be granted willingly by present leaders.

Even if it were possible to establish a central authority for some nations, ideologies, economies, and religions, it would still not be a "Mankind authority." It would lead neither to greater freedom for the people nor to greater unity for Mankind. On the contrary, it would serve to set up opportunities and instrumentalities for more cataclysmic wars, for more ruthless ideological conflicts, and for deeper hostilities between haves and have-nots. The years since the Second World War have provided ample evidence that by itself larger organization does not signify progress for Mankind. The agencies of cooperation—the United Nations, the Peace Corps, the International Geophysical Year, the Pugwash Conferences, the Ecumenical Council, Telstar, etc.—have been more than balanced by the hot wars, the cold wars, and all the other major conflicts of modern society. The conclusion seems inescapable that nothing less than a Mankind-oriented society is the solution for the problems of the people.

THE EVOLUTION OF MANKIND LEADERSHIP

It should not be expected that in a "Mankind society" the people would be set free at once. If in the past they were servants of a system, in the future they would still be servants of a system. The difference is that while the present system is segmental and the people serve the interests of one segment against those of another, the other system is universal and the people would serve the interests of all. While under previous systems they were obliged to sacrifice freedom, independence, and self-determination, under the Mankind system the people would still have to make sacrifices, but the sacrifices would concern the elimination of illiteracy, ignorance, inertia, and indifference. Although the people would still be dependent upon leadership, in the Mankind age it would be enlightened leadership.

168

How may an enlightened Mankind leadership be expected to evolve? Teilhard de Chardin sees the moral and spiritual process this way:

> If indeed an almost limitless field of action lies open to us in the future, what shall our moral dispositions be, as we contemplate this march ahead? I can think of two, which may be summarized in six words: *a great hope held in common.*

> First, the hope, this must spring to life spontaneously in every generous spirit faced by the task that awaits us; and it is also the essential *impulse,* without which nothing can be done. A passionate longing to grow, to be, is what we need. . . .

> A hope held in common. Here again the history of Life is decisive. Not all directions are good for our advance: one alone leads

upward, that which through increasing organization leads to greater synthesis and unity. . . .

How is the drawing together to be accomplished? *A priori*, there seem to be two methods, two possible roads.

The first is a process of tightening up in response to external pressures . . . The human mass, because on the confined surface of this planet it is in a state of continuous additive growth, in numbers and interconnections, must automatically become more and more tightly concentrated upon itself. . . .

But there is another way. This that, *prompted by some flavouring influence,* the elements of Mankind should succeed in making effective a profound force of mutual attraction, deeper and more powerful than the surface-repulsion which causes them to diverge. . . .

In my view the road to be followed is clearly revealed by the teaching of all the past. We can progress only by uniting: this, as we have seen, is the law of Life. But unification through coercion leads only to superficial pseudo-unity. . . . . Only unification through unanimity is biologically valid. This alone can work the miracle of causing heightened personality to emerge from the forces of collectivity. . . . Therefore it is inwardly that we must come together, and in entire freedom.[3]

The *dynamic* process of integration may present a different picture. The Center for Research on World Political Institutions at Princeton University points out that the integration of communities occurs in two basically different stages: a preparatory stage in which "political integration may be a matter for theorists, for writers, for a few statesmen, or a few small pressure groups"; and the stage after "take-off," when "integration is a matter of broad political movements, of governments, or of major interest groups, often an affair of more or less organized mass persuasion and mass response. . . . Before take-off, the proposal for integration is a matter of theory; after take-off, it is a political force."[4]

Finally, the *educational* process toward integration on a higher level is thus described by Robert Ulich, Professor Emeritus at Harvard University:

The primary need of higher education is to educate a person in whom the rational qualities and the loyalty to truth are so developed that they influence his whole judgment and conduct. If a student is unable to lift up his life standards by the vicarious participation in the thought and work of men who have directed Mankind's pursuit of truth, justice and happiness, he does not belong in an institution of higher education. Here may be the main link between the idea of the university and the idea of Mankind, and hence between higher education and the future of Mankind. Liberal education should deepen in students the awareness that, as human beings, they are a part of Mankind, not only in a numerical, but also in a spiritual sense. The more they learn themselves and about themselves, the more they should also learn about humanity."[5]

CONCLUSION

Little has been said about the people, yet all of this chapter is concerned with the people and their future. The accent here is on leadership, which is in accord with the historical truism that leaders will visualize and create, while the people will realize and translate vision into reality. Leadership must take the initial steps—in this as in any other major effort. The new world of freedom for the people (as for anyone else) must be envisioned and originated by a new leadership; but that leadership will emerge mostly from the broad ranks of the people and the middle class.

The basic motivation of new leadership usually derives from dissatisfaction with existing conditions. Therefore, new leadership will come not so much from those in positions of authority in existing institutions as from those in opposition to or rebellion against them; not so much from incumbent presidents, priests, and politicians as from advocates of social reform, economic equality, and political liberation. As history shows, new leadership is not likely to succeed unless it is supported by some of the ruling interests (see Chapter Two). It is the obvious task of Mankind leaderhip to blend the practical orientation with the future image of Mankind, to combine the realistic evaluation with the idealistic motivation.

170

The question arises whether Mankind leadership should originate in the segments that make up Mankind—nations, races, institutions, cultures, and disciplines. If so, how is it to establish the overarching premise on which all of them can build the orderly society? Or must it originate in the entity of Mankind that stands above the parts? If that is the case, how can it do justice to the diversity of existing associations and relationships throughout the world?

Only from its segments can Mankind leadership draw the infinite diversity of activities, beliefs, aspirations, and objectives. This diversity makes up the purposeful contents of human life and the meaningful totality of man's society. Without full participation of this global complex, Mankind leadership would float in the air—a spineless, meaningless collection of admonitions, regulations, and good intentions.

But only from the whole can Mankind leadership derive the overarching concept, the inspiration for global design, and the image of future Mankind. These qualities constitute the heart of the Mankind effort, without which it would have neither basic significance nor purposeful orientation.

It follows that Mankind leadership must arise simultaneously from within and from without the segments. It must work from within through nation, race, and culture toward a Mankind pattern and dimension. And it must work from without through new perspectives, new ideas, and new commitments toward a broadening of organizations and institutions.

Throughout history, new problems and new opportunities have given birth to new dynamic leadership. Although the contemporary age has created vast opportunities and enormous problems of the gravest urgency for all of Mankind, it has not yet produced dynamic Mankind leadership. Why not? Among many reasons, three of special significance may be cited:

(1) Our age is one of entirely new dimensions and perspectives. It requires basic rethinking and new understanding. It involves changes of the most profound nature. It demands transformations unparalleled in human history.

(2) Our age concerns all of the people in a single group. This fact

171

implies the need for thought and action on an unprecedented scale. It calls for leadership whose concern and compassion enclose the entire human world.

(3) Our age is under stress of great urgency and requires virtually immediate action on vast problems both novel and complex.

The three dimensions of change, space, and time indicate some of the obstacles blocking the rise of Mankind leadership. The demands on that leadership are much greater today than they ever were on any leadership in the past. It is more difficult to develop brand-new Mankind leadership than, for example, to rise against existing leadership; it means transcending it without destroying it. It is more difficult to create entirely new dimensions of organized living on a global scale than, for example, to create a new nation, because the basic principles and formulas for Mankind leadership exist only in the dimmest outline if at all. The actual need is to build a completely new framework in which Mankind leadership can grow effectively and act decisively.

172 Facing the terrifying prospect of Mankind grinding to a halt, we must not wait and wonder whether and when a Mankind leadership might arise somewhere in our midst. We must assume that a leadership of universal orientation and of dedication to Mankind has already gained reality in different parts of the globe but has so far remained undetected and unrecognized. We must demand of this leadership that it step forward, identify, and prove itself.

The basic question modern man must face and answer is whether new leadership forms, which in the past have proved effective in the segmental framework, can now prove themselves in the Mankind framework. The leadership of Mankind must be a leadership of universality. It cannot arise solely in the United States or the Congo, in China, Great Britain, India or Israel. If it did, more likely than not, before long it would slide into a quasi-segmental premise, acquire a segmental character (for identity's sake), and be directed against segmental opposition. American leadership of Mankind would not be recognized by all, nor would an Asian, African or any other continental, regional or racial leadership be so recognized.

Leadership on the universal Mankind level is one that transcends the limitations of national, racial or cultural identification. In order to avoid segmentalization, Mankind leadership must create an identity and an image that stands above and yet includes all others; that is distinct from all others and yet, in the sense of human striving, is like all others in that it is guided by human ideas, motivations and aspirations.

While the leadership of Mankind must work out its relations with nations, races, and religions; with labor, capital, and management; and with all other branches of human endeavor—it must above all clarify and put in order the significance and the priority of moral and spiritual values in the minds of men. It is here that the universality of man has a true foundation upon which the house of Mankind will be built—a house divided into many mansions but united by a single belief:—the belief in the dignity of man.

173

MANKIND
BELIEVERS:
AN
ACTION
PROGRAM

MANKIND
BELIEVERS:
AN
ACTION
PROGRAM

177

INTRODUCTION

The Second World War had again aroused man's desire for peace. When the atom bomb destroyed Hiroshima, desire flamed into determination that war must no longer be tolerated in modern civilization. The United Nations organization was an expression of this determination.

Amid the world-wide acclaim of anti-war movements, voices of skepticism were heard. Why should world peace be possible now when it had never been possible before? The answer that war could now destroy Western, perhaps all civilization, and that therefore the survival of all of us left no alternative to peace, did not satisfy the skeptics. If this were true, they said, why do nations keep arming, why is there no universal acceptance of the World Court, why do nations refuse to relinquish part of their sovereignty so as to make possible a world authority?

The further reply that this takes time and that in the end

the people shall prevail in their demand for a peaceful world was condemned as wishful thinking. Time will not solve the present crisis; more likely, it will increase tension. As for the people, they are controlled by leaders and the interests they represent. As a positive contribution, the skeptics pointed out that we really do not understand this age of crisis. While speaking freely about Mankind, we do not know what Mankind signifies, what part we are playing in it, or what part we (and all the other things that make up Mankind) might be expected to play in the future.

To find possible answers to these and related questions is the purpose of the Council for the Study of Mankind, Inc. It owes its beginnings in 1952 to a group of noted scholars, mostly of the University of Chicago, including Professors Richard P. McKeon and Charles Morris, both Philosophy; Quincy Wright, International Law; Robert Redfield, Anthropology; Herbert Blumer, Sociology; and also Adolf A. Berle, Law, Columbia University. They were soon joined by Hans Kohn, History, City College of New York; Theodore Brameld, Educational Philosophy, Boston University; Robert Ulich, Education, Harvard University; Bert F. Hoselitz, Economics, University of Chicago; and many others. The author of this book, Gerhard Hirschfeld, was appointed, and still serves, as its executive director.

The Council's main purpose is Mankind education. Because of the scarcity of educational material on the subject of Mankind, especially for teaching on the elementary and high-school level, the Council set about to produce its own material. It has held fifteen international conferences on various disciplines related to the concept of Mankind. They were followed by books, of which three have so far been published: *Education and the Idea of Mankind, Economics and the Idea of Mankind,* and *History and the Idea of Mankind,* with two more, *Technology and the Idea of Mankind* and *Toward a Mankind School,* about to be published. Ten monographs on the idea of Mankind have been prepared for classroom use on all levels of education, in addition to a large number of lectures, articles, and special papers.

What we did in the Council was good, but in my twenty years of organized Mankind work I often felt it was not good enough because it did not go far enough. With others, inside the Council and out, I shared a sense of inadequacy and, subsequently, a sense of urgency. Merely to study Mankind problems seemed only part of the task. What was to be done with the results? At which point, in what form, and to what extent and precise purpose was action called for?

The more I thought about it, the more I became convinced that an action program, dealing with Mankind's most pressing problems, was an urgent necessity. Those who believe in Mankind and its future, must take up a new initiative. They must set a straight course for what seems to me the ultimate goal: the creation of a Mankind-oriented society.

How might this task be realized? How should it be evaluated? What would be its rational foundation? And what its philosophy? What inner resources would be required? What outer form, design, and structure might be selected?

The following pages present my version of how the task might be approached. It is an initial effort arising from and, in a small way, responding to this sense of inadequacy and urgency.

MANKIND BELIEVERS

Two-thirds through the twentieth century, reckless materialism and unbridled nationalism reigned virtually unopposed throughout the world. If it was not open warfare in South-East Asia, it was hidden war in Latin America. If it was not poisoning of air and water, it was poisoning of people's minds. If it was not the rich getting richer, it was the poor staying as poor as ever. Moral and spiritual values carried on a precarious existence along the rim of society's trembling perimeter. Their voices were but faintly heard above the thundering noise of a turbulent world.

This was the situation as it appeared to some people who were growing increasingly concerned about the future of human society. There were many grave problems, but these people were not so much concerned about the gravity of the problems as about their incorrect evaluation. They wanted to know the truth. They felt:

Major problems are Mankind problems, requiring a Mankind approach rather than segmental approaches. *Mankind* should be the focus.

People are the basic issue rather than general theories, policies, philosophies, or ideologies.

Nevertheless, original solutions to actual problems must be sought on the *leadership* level rather than through the people.

These were some of the reasons why the concerned people were unable to fit their concern into any existing organization. While many groups were equally concerned, they were usually involved in many problems. The people here referred to recognized just one central problem: Mankind! They were ignorant about many aspects, but they felt sure of one thing: They believed in the reality of Mankind. They believed in it as a supreme value. They believed in its future. They called themselves: *Mankind Believers*

180   COMMON CHARACTERISTICS

Throughout the world, people are linked by many common characteristics:

Biologically: All people are of like origin, come from the same species, and are of the same basic substance.

Aspirationally: All people require satisfaction of the physical needs, share desire for improvement, need appreciation.

Spiritually: All people need a religious faith, live by moral standards, value personal pride and dignity.

As Professor Louis Gottschalk of The University of Chicago points out, there has been through the centuries a perceptible trend toward a world culture. Some of its discernible components are found in:

Biological Diffusion: The migrations of foods, peoples, and disease.

Technological Diffusion: The generalized use of arts and crafts, cloths, ceramics, paper and printing, navigational instruments, gunpowder, and modern technology.

Religious Diffusion: The spread of Buddhism, Confucianism, Stoicism, Christianity, Jewish Diaspora, Islam, and modern missions.

Political Diffusion: The course of empires, exploration, the idea of Rights of Man, self-determination, spread of Marxism, and concept of world citizenship.

Economic Diffusion: The spread of mercantilism, laissez-faire, international banking, multi-national corporations, "bourgeois" ethics, and philanthropy.

Arts and Letters Diffusion: The borrowings in the fine arts, literary migrations, architectural interchange, and musical diffusions.

Sciences Diffusion: The universality of modern science, multi-national scientific enterprises, international scientific academies and societies.[1]

FAITH

Notwithstanding its living reality, Mankind is basically a matter of faith. So is the nation basically a matter of faith, however realistic its existence, history, interests, and aspirations may be. The person who lacks faith in the nation is not likely to contribute significantly to its growth, power, and prestige. So with Mankind.

Mankind derives its singular significance from the fact that it is the greatest of temporal institutions. It offers far larger and richer opportunities than have been known in the past. Their exploitation calls for creativity and inventiveness of a new order and scope. For this task, faith is indispensable.

There is no precedent for a Mankind-oriented society. Men and women will be challenged to produce new ideas, methods, forms, designs, and dimensions for the creation and operation of a novel complex of interconnected societies. To think about it creatively, to work on it consistently, to teach it conscientiously, one must have faith in it.

COMMITMENT

To signify its Mankind orientation, faith must express itself in tangible form. This form may be a sense of responsibility toward Mankind, or it may be a precise commitment to serve the interest of Mankind in every possible way. Believers will choose the latter as the proper expression of their faith. Indeed, going beyond the mere declaration of a commitment, they may insist that to be meaningful commitment must be accompanied by representative action.

The Mankind world having the greatest potential of all material worlds, no major compromise would be either logical or even possible. Unless Mankind is accepted as the primary concept, it cannot meaningfully represent the totality of man and his society. The foundation of the Mankind concept is its universality. Relegated to the rank of *primus inter pares*, Mankind would acquire a segmental character, thus losing its universality along with its primary identification. To remain true to its character as well as to its promise, Mankind must have primary allegiance.

Nor does "serving the interest of Mankind" simply mean working for law and order, peace and international cooperation. These conditions exist in many countries. What does not exist are the conditions of the Mankind framework: *world* law, *world* order, *world* peace, and *world* cooperation. Hence, grave and urgent problems are confronting human society. The commitment of Believers "to serve the interest of Mankind," is to relate, to evaluate, and to attack all major problems and issues where they belong: in the framework of Mankind.

LEARNING

Believers must first educate themselves so they will understand the new conditions and help other people to understand them. Many people have faith in and a sense of responsibility to Mankind: housewives volunteer work at clinic and hospital; physicians seek to restore the health of their patients; lawyers work on cases involving the public interest; poets sing of the beauty of nature. In short, millions of people the world over perform fine services for their fellow men. Their work helps alleviate suffering, improve community life, advance the interests of state and nation, and create beauty.

This is great work. But for Mankind it is not enough. However admirable the dedication of housewives, physicians, lawyers, poets, and many others, their work does not bear upon the issues facing twentieth-century Mankind. Their noble work could have been done (as in fact it was done, if under different circumstances) in the fourteenth century AD or the fourth century BC. It was done in every age in human history because human needs demanded it.

In the contemporary age, the problems of Mankind are greater than the daily needs of man. There are basic things necessary to the attainment of the Mankind-oriented society which Believers, and an increasing number of other people, must learn to get used to. Perhaps none is more important than getting used to thinking in a new perspective:

> They must learn to think about changing conditions next week, next month, next year—not in the perspective of community or nation only, but in that of Mankind.

> They must learn to think in the new perspective about the kind of world in which they would want their children to build a good life in a good society.

> They must learn to think in the new perspective about the changing character of neighborhoods—black, brown, yellow, white, mixed.

> They must learn to think in the new perspective about the policies their nation ought to pursue in the conflict of global issues.

> They must learn to think in the new perspective about changing spiritual values.

> In short, they must learn to think about these and many other issues

IN THE PERSPECTIVE OF MANKIND.

PERSPECTIVE

New conditions change perspectives. The forces that upset conditions throughout the world deeply affected people's lives. At first, when the storm crushed century-old systems, institutions, and traditions, people attended to their lives as dictated by custom. Now that the storm has drawn their private world into its vortex, people must reorientate themselves to find their place of responsibility, of meaning, of value, and, last but not least, of dignity in the world of tomorrow.

As Believers adapt themselves to new conditions, they see new perspectives change the nature and with it the emphasis of major problems. If people deal with national problems, Believers point out, they look at them in the perspective of the nation, that is, in the light of the particular situation, aspiration, and primary interest of the nation. If people deal with Mankind problems, they might be expected to look at them in the light of the particular situation, aspiration, and primary interest of Mankind. But this is not the case. And here is the rub, because the difference between the perspective of nation and of Mankind is not only very real, it is crucial.

Take *Education*. In the United States, the most important problems concern desegregation, the alarming drop-out rate of high school students, and federal subsidies to private and parochial schools. Shifting to the viewpoint of developing nations in Asia, Africa, Latin America, whose populations constitute a larger part of Mankind, entirely different problems dominate the scene: difficulties of communication and transportation, high rates of illiteracy, and a lack of funds for even the most modest educational training and schooling facilities. Obviously, what might be done to solve the educational problems of the nation should not be done to solve those of Mankind.

Take *Medical Care*. Among the outstanding problems in the United States are the constantly rising cost of medical care, the equally rising cost of supporting the growing aged population, and the spreading calamity of mental illness. In contrast, the most pressing problems in the medical care field in the developing nations include the largely uncontrolled population explosion, the slow progress of the organized fight against disease, and the survival not only of the fittest but of the least fit—with all its social, economic, and political implications. Again, the effective approach to the solution of the nation's problems in medical care is basically different from the effective approach to the solution of Mankind's problems.

Take *Automation*. In highly developed economies such as the United States, automation often creates problems of massive unemployment, the estrangement of workers from their jobs, and an undermining of personal values. All of these may cause serious dislocations in personal attitudes and social adjustment. In developing nations, automation creates different problems: for example, how to build an automated industry on top of an often poorly developed semi-agricultural economy; how to balance largely undeveloped resources against the soaring ambitions of new-born nationalism; how to protect ancient cultures, traditions, beliefs, and values against the impact of technological inventions. The tools and methods designed for the American environment do not generally show the same results when applied to basically different conditions in less developed countries.

Take *Freedom*. The American interpretation of freedom differs from that of, say, the Chinese. Both might differ from the Mankind interpretation, which would embrace all kinds of freedom. In a pluralistic society, which a Mankind system by its very nature would have to be, there would be room for more than one interpretation of freedom.

Believers conclude that the choice of perspectives is decisive in the judgment of Mankind problems. Continued use of present perspectives is more likely to hinder than to help the solution of Mankind problems. They are critical of the belief held by some that new perspectives can be attained merely by broadening existing dimensions. If you change dimensions, they point out, you do not change either principle or perspective.

When in the past, Great Britain, France, the United States, and other powers acquired vast overseas territories in Asia, Africa, Latin America, and Oceania, they did not automatically attain either Mankind principles or Mankind perspectives. Nor would the wider distribution of world resources necessarily cause nations to moderate their aspirations and international interests in order to pursue more peaceful policies. On the contrary, due to greater equality in military strength and economic resources, even more bitter, more expanded, and more determined conflict might take place. The long-term historical experience shows that greater concentration of power on the one side provokes a parallel development on the other (see European history during the last two centuries).

INADEQUACIES

In the East as in the West, people are not prepared to meet the new conditions. Brought up in partisan identifications, they are taught to think as Americans or Japanese, as Christians or Jews, Buddhists or Moslems, Democrats or Communists. As a result, they interpret beliefs and aspirations of other people in the light of their own indoctrination. The majority are tied to long-established values, traditions, languages, and relationships. To loosen these ties so as to make room for the awareness of Mankind would require strong determination and painful reorientation.

It is then no surprise that the general attitude toward international cooperation is hardly encouraging. After fifty years of dedicated efforts, first by the League of Nations, then by United Nations, talk about Mankind is still circuitous. Direct confrontation with Mankind as an indivisible entity rather than as a patchwork of confused and confusing nations, races, and institutions is still avoided. Mankind has yet to prove its ability to become an effectively operating global organization.

The task of adapting to the new conditions is made more difficult by the fact that so little is known about Mankind and its impact upon nation, community, family, and ourselves. There is no science of Mankind. If institutions of learning were asked to relate certain disciplines to Mankind, they would find it difficult to carry out the assignment. Nor would jurists find it possible at this time to design and put into effect an operative law for Mankind; they would lack the necessary knowledge and experience, not to mention the indispensable authority supported by world-wide agreement.

Should it occur to people to jump with both feet onto the greener acres of Mankind with an oath of loyalty and an affirmation of commitment, they would find it difficult to locate either flag or constitution, either codes or statutes to guide their way. By the same token, any effort to develop a standard of ethics for Mankind would likely be frustrated by the prevailing ignorance of the multiple associations and relationships that make up the totality of Mankind.

As a result, institutions on virtually every level of education throughout the world lack a curriculum on the subject of Mankind as an indivisible entity, as an overarching concept, and as the primary value in the survival of civilization. The general awareness of Mankind is thus grossly inadequate throughout the world.

Despite the fact that the advance of science and technology makes Mankind awareness virtually a pre-requisite for survival; despite the fact that people are challenged to adjust to life in a new world; despite the fact that they are aware of other nations, other races, and other people; and despite the fact that they see constant improvements in communication and transportation, shrinking the human orbit to ever smaller dimensions, the fact remains that, if all these awarenesses are added up, they still do not amount to the awareness of Mankind. They are partial and parochial; Mankind is universal. One can no better understand a symphony from the twelve tones of the scale, or a chemical compound from its atoms, than one can understand Mankind from its farms and factories, airports and harbors, nations and cities. Nothing short of the realization of human society as a solid entity can impart the awareness of Mankind.

Equally inadequate is the connection between the parts (nations, races, institutions) and the whole (Mankind). None of the parts can deal with the whole of Mankind. No single part can solve the problems of Mankind. No single nation (or bloc of nations) can abolish war between nations. No single bank can underwrite the financial needs of developing nations. No single educational association can solve world illiteracy. No single group can deal effectively with poverty, population, pollution, inflation, automation, drug addiction, and other problems. Only the combined resources of Mankind will prove equal to the task; only full cooperation can provide the needed resources.

187

In educating themselves and others, the Believers may face two basic questions that contain the key to the solution of Mankind problems: one deals with the awareness, the other with the understanding of the concept of Mankind.

AWARENESS AND UNDERSTANDING

To Believers, the major difference is that Mankind awareness does not have any special meaning, while Mankind understanding has. The idea that Mankind today offers greater wealth and opportunity than ever before represents a kind of Mankind awareness. It may be an interesting observation, but to most people who have this idea it would not be particularly meaningful.

However, if some of these people would see not only the greater wealth, variety, and opportunity but also the greater problems and crises, and if they realized that in order to evaluate this greater whole they need to think in larger perspectives, then they would have a kind of Mankind understanding. Because then, thanks to their ability to interpret events, to draw implications, and to form judgments, the observation would become meaningful to them.

In contrast, Believers say, Mankind awareness is watchfulness in observing, which permits the idea of Mankind to enter a person's mind. It means he becomes alive to the existence of Mankind; it does not mean the idea becomes meaningful. Believers might illustrate the distinction between Mankind awareness and Mankind understanding by using a practical example, like:

FOOD IN THE WORLD ECONOMY

In manifold stages of operation, when would food involve Mankind awareness, and at which point involve Mankind understanding? Believers might see the process this way:

When a person is aware
that many people eat
different kinds of food
in many different ways

also, that some people
  eat very little food,
    or hardly any food at all,
      and let it go at that . . .

that is Mankind awareness, requiring neither motivation nor particular interest nor judgment.

But when, in addition, a person finds out

Not only that many developing countries
  produce sufficient crops
    to feed their population,

But also that they export food
  to obtain foreign exchange,
    rather than saving it
      for home consumption,

Not only that they often use revenue
  to build up automated industry,
    for which they are not ready,

But also that people have false ideas
  of getting rich quick
    through skilled jobs in industry,

  abandoning in the process
    ancient traditions and values,
      difficult to replace,

then he has Mankind understanding, because:

(a) he shows Mankind interest, motivation, and judgment;

(b) he sees interaction between some of the parts that make up Mankind;

(c) he has a glimpse of the totality of Mankind and some of its interrelated functions; and

(d) Mankind has become meaningful to him.

189

The more advanced the Mankind idea, the broader must be the Mankind understanding. There is, for example, the notion held by Believers that the Mankind concept stands quite alone, that it has no direct precedent that can be followed in trying to realize its potential, that its far-reaching significance cannot be comprehended within existing patterns of thought. This notion implies that a fuller understanding of Mankind must grow from new thoughts and new visions.

Another implication, equally important to Believers, suggests that the value of Mankind is greater than that of any other material thing. The success or failure of dealing with the vast promises and urgent problems of Mankind involves the survival not only of Western but perhaps of all civilization. Man should therefore be willing to make greater sacrifices in the cause of Mankind than in any other cause.

Whatever the implication, Mankind awareness is the obvious prerequisite. There can be no Mankind understanding without Mankind awareness. But awareness is only the beginning. We must set goals, say Believers, for the understanding of Mankind. They think a person has that understanding:

> When he understands the reasons why Mankind is more important than any or all nations, any or all races, any or all religions, institutions, disciplines, cultures, or civilizations: because Mankind is all of these.

> When he understands that Mankind is every human being—and all human beings; every individual creature—and all human creatures: past, present, and future.

> When he understands why people find it difficult to understand Mankind. People derive meaning from the particular rather than the general. They become attached to what to them has meaning: home, family, job, friends, community, or nation. What they are not attached to, like Mankind, does not find ready understanding.

> When he understands that major problems are Mankind problems. Great dangers have arisen to the particular: the individual person, the family, and the community. But the greater dangers are rooted in the general: threat of global nuclear war, the problems of pollution, population, poverty, education, drug addiction, inflation, automation, loss of identity, fading values, and many others. They now affect (or soon will) most people around the world. They are Mankind problems.

> When he understands that the idea and vision of Mankind are blurred by the many segments that make up its totality. In order to understand Mankind, people must learn to transcend segmental

limitations imposed on their thinking by national, racial, cultural, institutional, and other influences.

When he understands that the protection of the integrity and the dignity of the individual person is one of Mankind's prime responsibilities.

When he develops a feeling for Mankind. When he asks of every major issue or problem: "How will if affect Mankind?" When on every basic question he puts the interests of Mankind first, his own second. When, guided by Mankind feeling, he knows as a fact that Mankind exists. When he can bring these and related feelings and attitudes into a Mankind relationship.

Then, he shall find his true identification, not primarily as a member of nation, race, or other segment but first of all as a member of Mankind.

THE NEW EFFORT

Human society is anchored in its institutions. But institutions are not anchored in human habits, be they thoughts or deeds. Believers realize that existing institutions are not equipped to deal effectively with today's major problems. Institutions, they would say, cannot be blamed for their shortcomings. They can be slow in their development (like twentieth-century democracy) or rapid (like the modern black movement), efficient (like some corporations) or wasteful (like some bureaucracies), timid or bold, brilliant or dull—depending upon the kind of thinking that guides their objectives and activities. If Believers decided that modern institutions needed to be enlarged, it should mean that the underlying thinking needed to be enlarged. If basic thinking were developed in larger perspectives, institutions would respond. Therefore, Mankind leadership should concentrate upon broader thinking, the results of which would gradually be passed on to institutions. Indeed, recent activities, newly directed toward broader understanding, are taking place in virtually all major branches of the human endeavor:

NEW ART

Many groups of artists and groups of styles are emerging in different parts of the world that are not allied with national groups. A quality of art is emerging which, transcending national styles, knows no geographical or temporal distinctions. Artists everywhere open their experience to the discovery of new, non-national, lines. Their works fall into constantly changing groupings out of which arises an expanding intellectual élite, which will be able to communicate on a broader and higher level.

Mankind, it has been said, is a mode of communication, in which one important factor is the perception of new art forms. In his book *The Rise of the West*, William McNeill indicates that it is the art object rather than music or literature that has been most easily diffused from one people to another. The universal aspect of art seems to make it easy for nations to assimilate forms that have originated in a specific locale. The continued development of non-national, cross-cultural art has thus great potential in stimulating the awareness of the universality of the Mankind concept.[2]

NEW ECONOMICS

World-wide agreements between corporations, organized labor, and government agencies are operating by the scores within the framework of the greater human society. World trade is receiving a powerful impetus from the growing merger of technical know-how and scientific management in advanced countries with production and distribution facilities, investment deals and labor contracts in developing countries.

Citing many examples of East-West industrial, managerial, technical, and financial cooperation, noted economist Emile Benoit says: "Such enormous, virtually permanent, worldwide organizations as General Motors, Jersey Standard, Unilever, Philips' Gloeilampen, etc., with assets and life expectations paralleling those of nation-states, completely transcend the competitive-market assumptions of classical economics."[3]

A new effort is the recent formation by Italian industrialist Aurelio Peccei of a group of scientists, economists, educators and businessmen, known as the "Club of Rome." Its studies apply the systems dynamics method in a computer simulation model of global interactions of population, natural resources, pollution, capital, and food production.[4]

NEW EDUCATION

Exchanges of teachers and students are taking place on a world-wide scale. Activities of UNESCO and related agencies in expanding teacher education facilities and programs in developing countries have grown substantially. In these activities, the World Bank, United Nations Development Program, and voluntary contributions from member nations and private agencies are playing an important part. Scholars in Western universities are pressing forward their studies in basic disciplines on a universal plane. Particular attention is paid to the humanities, and they continue to grow more important in the curriculum. Scholars project their data-gathering techniques and interpreting procedures into heretofore neglected non-Western areas, nations, and cultures.

While it is doubtful whether at the present time any institution can be called a world university, a number of institutions approximate the concept of complete internationality and if developed further could become genuine world universities. An example is Friends World College in Long Island, New York. Other institutions in the Eastern as well as the Western Hemisphere may soon appear. A growing school holds that the understanding of Man kind depends on man's ability to transcend himself and identify with others; to develop human beings who act on the basis of their belief in and concern for man and Mankind.

NEW RELIGION

Many churchmen throughout the world engage increasingly in dialogue with decision-makers in the power structure, to make them aware of their moral responsibilities as they bear not only upon the welfare but the survival of human society.

Three movements indicate a trend toward more universal orientation:

(1) The ecumenical movement emphasizes the pursuit of common goals of universal scope; it finds expression in the various

decisions of the Ecumenical Council. While the movement has found growing approval and support, it has also encountered criticism. Increasingly, it has been asked: "Why should one stop with *Christian* unity?"

(2) The post-ecumenical movement features the inter-religious community. It foreshadows an age (in the words of Professor Willard Gurdon Oxtoby, Yale University) "when the world of experience and reality, which theology will have to interpret for Christians, will be a world with horizons far beyond the Judeo-Christian."[5]

(3) The third movement is developing on campuses, in institutions, and in communities throughout the world. Known as "United Religion," "Religious Pluralism," "Religious World Community," and other names, it is perhaps the most spontaneous of the religious movements in that it follows no fixed pattern, tradition, or doctrine. While in many respects it is highly individualistic, in a basic sense it seems to follow a universal orientation.

NEW SCIENCE

A number of scientific programs have been tried with broad international cooperation. One of the most successful was the International Geophysical Year; one of its major results was the Antarctic Treaty which put six million square miles of earth under international agreement. Another major achievement was the signing of the Atomic Test Ban, made possible by world-wide cooperation of scientists. A series of international conferences is engaged in the planning, design, and organization of space exploration on the one hand and of the exploitation of oceanic resources on the other. In developing new ideas and programs of world-wide scope, the Pugwash and related conferences play an important role. Scientists from different parts of the world give the discussions a global orientation. Attention is paid to the need to make results available to all nations.

The implications of such innovations as the computer system and automation as instruments in the reordering of the affairs of human society are far-reaching, but uncertain. Both are being used increasingly on a world-wide basis. But whether their short-term benefits will outweigh the problems they are likely to create over a longer period of time can probably be answered only when the results have been brought in by Mankind itself. Certainly, the assumption of infinite technological growth must not be taken for granted.

This brief summary is a small sample of the many activities going on around the globe on behalf of world cooperation. Mostly taken from American sources, the information omits regional activities in many parts of the world—in the communist countries, in developing nations in Asia, Africa, Latin America, and parts of Europe. Even so, the summary shows that these efforts for the benefit of human society surpass anything done in any previous age. Never before have so many people been involved in programs designed to benefit all. Never before have plans been drawn on such a gigantic scale. Never before have they engaged the attention of so many statesmen, experts, and specialists, as well as intellectual and spiritual leaders, and creators of public opinion. Never before has the expressed concern for Mankind formed so intimate a part of the daily affairs of Mankind.

However, upon closer study of these and similar efforts, it will become apparent to Mankind Believers that, while many may have been originally motivated by concern for the future of human society, few seem to have been made actually in the awareness of Mankind, let alone in the primary consideration of Mankind's special interests. While in many cases they represent notable advances toward world enlightenment and, hopefully, world unity, they can hardly be called true Mankind efforts. Some may benefit Mankind; others may have results that could hardly have been anticipated and that may actually be harmful to Mankind.

In *new art,* the movement of universality may fall victim to a confused diversity of misconceived art forms or it may continue its development of non-national, cross-cultural art and thus of its great potential in stimulating the awareness of the idea of Mankind.

In *new economics,* world-wide agreements between corporations, labor unions, and government agencies may as easily serve nations preparing for war as developing nations improving transportation facilities.

In *new education,* teacher and student exchange may in some cases cause or intensify discord and violence and in other cases contribute substantially to better understanding.

In *new religion,* the ecumenical movement may be obstructed or destroyed by inter-religious rivalries or be advanced by a growing spirit of world religious community.

In *new science,* a program like the Antarctic Treaty may be exploited by narrow national interests or may lead to other agreements of a similar nature.

Observing these and other characteristics, Believers may conclude that, as a means toward the attainment of world unity, the new effort was lacking in two vital elements: Mankind focus and Mankind support.

The new effort does not seem to be generally concerned with a single (that is, a Mankind) focus but with several focuses; in fact, many efforts may not even identify Mankind as a major target. Yet, Believers think that in making progress toward the creation of a Mankind-oriented society a Mankind focus should be considered of prime importance. Without it, the effort would hang in the air, having no anchor to hold it in place. Lacking definite orientation, it would tend to go off in all directions—as, indeed, it is doing now, emitting many sparks but starting no fire.

196 Again, without a Mankind focus, segmental approaches would tend to be accepted as quasi-universal solutions rather than being relegated to the overarching concept. This would make for commitment to parochial and partisan causes rather than insisting upon commitment to the central cause. In short, the Mankind focus would assure anchor, direction, and the overarching concept as well as commitment to the universal task.

As to Mankind support, it is doubtful whether any of the aforementioned efforts indicate permanent support on a broad scale. Nor do they seem particularly concerned with the people, their interests, or their problems. Where leadership establishes broad coordination, it does not succeed in the principle of coordination (which is what Mankind needs), but only in a specific project, as in the International Geophysical Year.

The achievements of the new effort are largely a result of individual inspiration and initiative. If they are to have an enduring impact upon Mankind, they need to be planned, designed, and organized upon a Mankind foundation in a Mankind framework along Mankind principles.

LEADERSHIP OF BELIEVERS

Such impact, Believers are likely to reason, could be attained only through a permanently coordinated global effort. Leaders would be needed to determine new goals, aspirations, and values; and to create new methods, tools, and designs through which to attain them. People would be needed to make the new methods, tools, and designs a part of their daily life, thereby making them a reality. However, people cannot play their part until leaders have prepared the way.

Mankind Believers would elect a leadership group of imaginative and responsible men and women. The criterion would not be nationality, race, color, creed, sex, or age, but faith in and commitment to Mankind as an indivisible whole and the ability to evaluate major issues and problems in the perspective of Mankind. The ability for leadership would be determined as much by the depth of insight and compassion as by the quality of education, knowledge, and experience.

The leadership group would seek to stimulate and to help decide action on major issues, but would refrain from taking action itself, that is, executing decisions and carrying out programs. The basic objective of the group would be to make the Mankind idea and interest the prime consideration in all major issues and problems.

Mankind projects should probably not be given the highest priority. As previously mentioned, the new art, economics, education, religion, science, and other disciplines already feature many projects of large international scope. Instead, the leadership group might concentrate on two primary tasks:

(1) Determining the most effective means of broadening the international into a global effort.

(2) Discovering methods by which broad segmental efforts be converted into Mankind efforts.

That Mankind problems can be discussed with representatives of leadership groups in different parts of the world has been amply demonstrated over the last twenty years by such organizations as the Council for the Study of Mankind, Inc.

What is yet to be shown is whether representatives of leadership groups in industry, agriculture, labor, science, finance, government, and other key segments of human society can be induced to go beyond study and discussion; whether they can be expected to respond to the grave challenge of our times by taking coordinated action on these self-same problems of global scope in the interest, the perspective, and the framework of Mankind.

COORDINATED PROCEDURE

In pursuit of its basic objective (to make the Mankind idea the primary consideration in all major issues), the leadership group would seek to coordinate, with similarly oriented groups, programs on Mankind's most urgent problems—

chiefly on three levels: Economic, Cultural, and Political.

Principal areas on the *economic* level are:

Productivity and Technology
Marketing and the Consumer
Communication, Transportation, Finance

Principle areas on the *cultural* level are:

Education and World History
Science-Technology, and the Arts
Morality and Philosophy

Principal areas on the *political* level are:

Organization ⎫
Education   ⎬ of Political Action
Direction   ⎭

ECONOMIC

In discerning the most effective means of broadening the international programs into a global effort, the leadership group might consider factors responsible for the successful cooperation attained in different segments of the world economy. Scientific technology, servo-mechanisms, corporate management, service industries, communications media, and other segments of the economy would not have enjoyed their brilliant success over a sustained period of time without a highly coordinated team effort focused on research, discovery, and development.

The leadership group would then realize that success was due to the ability of leaders in management, labor, science, technology, and other branches to bring special resources to bear upon the exploitation of opportunities in particular fields. Conversely, it would realize that the ineffectiveness of the Mankind effort was due to the inability of persons in authority to concentrate adequate resources upon the attainment of objectives of high priority in the global arena where the concept of Mankind is leading a precarious existence. In order to bring effective techniques into the Mankind effort, the leadership group might ask in regard to:

TECHNOLOGY ASSESSMENTS
Why is the multi-discipline "systems approach," which is well suited to making technology assessments,
NOT APPLIED TO MANKIND ENTERPRISE?

SPECIALIZED DEVICES
Why are such devices as "Feedback Mechanism" or "Delphi Technique"
NOT APPLIED TO MANKIND ENTERPRISE?

RESEARCH ON INNOVATIONS
Why is continuing experimental research, which is needed to ascertain the direct impacts as well as the side effects of major social and technological innovations,
NOT APPLIED TO MANKIND ENTERPRISE?

MODERN PLANNING PROCEDURE

Why is not modern planning procedure, which provides a set of common goals for various laboratories, that is, a forecast of probable future systems, such as is used by the U.S. Air Force and other large organizations,

NOT APPLIED TO MANKIND ENTERPRISE?

SOPHISTICATED MANAGEMENT

Why is management practice, where drive for uninterrupted growth bars emotion from blocking efficiency, and where sacrifices are made to assure the attainment of fixed goals,

NOT APPLIED TO MANKIND ENTERPRISE?

EDUCATION AND TRAINING

Why is careful, detailed attention, which has shown remarkable results in enlightened educational systems,

in exemplary use of educational TV,
in high averages in science and mathematics
in USA, USSR, Japan, other countries,

NOT APPLIED TO MANKIND ENTERPRISE?

STRICT PRINCIPLES

200

Why are principles such as:
Good Pay for Good Work!
Neither Favors nor Privileges!
Sole Criterion: Qualification and Fitness for Job!

NOT APPLIED TO MANKIND ENTERPRISE?

In its effort to broaden the economic into a Mankind effort, the leadership group would seek to interest international organizations in joint action. In the area of food, for example, it might seek the cooperation of groups such as the Food and Agriculture Organization in persuading authorities in advanced as well as developing nations to work out assistance plans in the framework of world food programs. Advanced nations would play an important part, of course. But developing nations would play another part which would be no less important because it would be smaller. The goal would be to lay the groundwork for coordinated and controlled world food productivity, marketing, and finance.

In another global area, that of the Multi-National Corporation, the leadership group might seek the cooperation of heads of large corporations and labor organizations in discussing, in the Mankind perspective, the economic relationship between highly developed and newly developing nations. In the past, world economic expansion came mostly from highly developed nations. One of the basic problems facing the leadership group would be how to get developing nations started on a productivity process on a substantial scale. What would be their obligation towards the organization of world productivity? And what the obligation of highly developed to less developed nations? It would fall to the leadership group to press for decisions and commitments, and to help make proper arrangements for their effective implementation.

As suggested by Professor Neil Jacoby, School of Business Administration, University of California in Los Angeles, the role of multinational business corporations in raising productivity might fall into four main categories:

(1) Rising Productivity the Key to Economic Progress in Developing Countries:

   (a) Manhours worked and output-per-manhour as factors in growth of Gross National Product

   (b) Primary components of productivity gains
       i) capital
       ii) education and training
       iii) other

(2) Roles of External Agencies in Raising Productivity:

   (a) Role of Agency for International Development and other unilateral aid agencies

   (b) Role of UN Special Fund, World Bank and multilateral agencies

   (c) Role of developing countries

(3) The Multinational Business Corporation as a Worldwide Agency of Productivity Enhancement:

   (a) Through its branch and subsidiary operations in developing countries

(b) Through its purchasing and selling activities

(c) Through the contacts of its foreign executives in developing countries

(4) How the Multinational Corporation can Magnify its Influence upon Productivity Gains:

(a) Means to enhance its influence upon local government

(b) Means to enhance its influence upon local businessmen

(c) Means to enhance its influence upon local farmers

(d) Means to enhance its influence upon local agencies of foreign aid.[6]

In a similar way, the Mankind group would seek the cooperation of other Mankind-oriented leadership groups, representing institutions old and new, disciplines formal and informal, nations developed and developing, ideologies conservative and liberal, civilizations East and West. With their active and often leading participation, the Mankind group would apply the most advanced ideas, methods, and instruments to deal effectively with Mankind's most urgent economic problems.

EDUCATION

Believers would see the main objectives of education, firstly, in the creation and, secondly, in the global development of a Mankind Education Program. To the two essential ingredients—the understanding of the Mankind concept and the development of the Mankind perspective—they would want to add another ingredient, the element of action—Mankind action.

Without action operating as a central force, the concept may easily become an abstraction which has neither face nor focus. Besides, the difficulty of handling a concept as evasive as that of Mankind may turn an originally highly creative approach into a routine that is easier to follow, but that also has the tendency to flatten out the longer one follows it. Finally, without the element of action, the understanding of the Mankind concept and the development of the Mankind perspective may become over-intellectualized.

People interested in the creation of a Mankind-oriented society will stress the goals one should strive for; among them:

> that human life must be valued and preserved;

> that the worth and dignity of the individual person must be respected;

> that human expectations and personal capabilities must be fully realized;

> that social order must be based on justice and the rule of Mankind values;

> that human association must be characterized by liberty and freedom;

> that Mankind conditions and values must take precedence over personal desires;

> that truth and knowledge must be desired and sought.

Believers will want to make sure *that* these excellent intentions will be carried out, and *how* they will be carried out. This will require a new effort, aiming at a carefully planned, diligently prepared, well-disciplined system of organized action—on the educational, cultural, and political level.

This effort will make Mankind education more than an educational program, more than education in the formal sense. It will make the teacher of a Mankind curriculum more than a teacher; he will become carrier of a new message, spokesman for a new era. It will make the student of a Mankind curriculum more than a student; he will become participant in a great new adventure.

This will call for a new dimension of personal involvement through active participation in the program, firm dedication to the task, and clear commitment to Mankind. It would not be so important to argue the various points again and again. It would be of primary importance to test them, to apply them, to *do* them.

In launching the Mankind Education Program, the Mankind leadership group, in cooperation with other educational leadership groups, might select the study of Mankind education methods for its first project. A number of methods would be analyzed as they are tested under varying conditions in selected schools in different countries throughout the world. This inquiry would lead to a study of criteria for Mankind textbooks, Mankind readers, and Mankind teaching materials in general. Finally, the project should give some attention to the larger aims of Mankind education. Says Professor Robert Ulich, Emeritus, Harvard University:

> All the great teachers of mankind aimed at something more profound than mere instruction, acquisition of knowledge, usefulness, and efficiency. Rather, they believed that education, through widening man's intellectual horizon, should at the same time lead him deeper into his own self—and this not merely for the purpose of developing his individuality but of helping him to discover the unity of his own striving with the strivings, hopes, and ideals, and also the loneliness, the sins, sufferings, and the aggressive tendencies, of all mankind. [7]

According to Professor Ulich, three qualities are essential to broader human understanding. The first is the quality of faith, the second the quality of self-transcendence, the third the quality of vision—all three disciplined and purified by reason and self-criticism. The leadership group might consider qualities such as these essential to a philosophy of Mankind education.

The results of this comprehensive study should be made available to a World Education Council which would present them in a program broad enough, basic enough, and practical enough to fit Mankind education needs and rights of all people regardless of age, sex, race, creed or nationality.

Perhaps the greatest challenge to the leadership group would come with the need to give people (young and not-so-young, rich and poor, literate and illiterate) a solid understanding of the new world, the Mankind world. It is this world for which they would be educated and which they would be called upon to convert from blueprint and design to application and reality.

Providing such an educational basis would be the fulfillment of one of the most important educational objectives of Mankind Believers: to enable people, after necessary training and under appropriate guidance, to develop an intelligence and a judgment which would play a decisive part in dealing effectively with Mankind's most urgent challenge: to wipe out, or at least to reduce substantially, the tragic effects of uncontrolled population growth, pollution, poverty, drug addiction, and other major problems.

WORLD HISTORY

Particularly relevant to Mankind education would be world history. The leadership group would be aware that, as Western civilization is only one of many civilizations, Western history is only one of many histories. It would also realize that, while world history is generally taught with a Western bias, attempts (as in UNESCO history) are now being made to correct this bias.

The leadership group would urge the preparation of world history in a true Mankind perspective as a task of the first importance. It would stress the need to prepare the ground carefully before so complex and comprehensive a project, combining unbiased world history with a world history curriculum in a Mankind education program, could be sucessfully undertaken.

The principal difficulty would be to establish a unified approach to the presentation of world history in a Mankind perspective. The solution to this problem would not require more learning of world history as much as a better balance through better understanding of the Mankind perspective and its meaning. If, in this sense, world history preparation might take the form of Mankind preparation, then historians might have a ready premise upon which to develop a unified approach.

Some of the stages of the world history project might be:

(1) Forming a special Mankind study group of historians who not only enjoy professional distinction, but also are sympathetic toward the aspiration of Mankind Believers.
(2) Forming a leadership group of educators, statesmen, students, parents, and advisors to consider the total project.
(3) Developing educational materials and preparing curriculum outlines.
(4) Organizing seminar discussions in different countries, submitting results to a World History Council for global action.
(5) Subsequent projects should gradually evolve toward the writing of a true world or, more precisely, Mankind history.

SCIENCE-TECHNOLOGY

206

Believers feel that their affinity to the idea of Mankind would be strengthened by a rapprochement between the natural and the social sciences; that it would lead to greater consideration of the former by the latter, and vice versa. Technology, for the first time, has given the human race the means to destroy itself; but also, for the first time, man can recognize a right to live common to all, and the right of all to benefit from the advances of science, technology, and culture.

Technology is basically tied to the culture from which it emerges. Our concern must be not only with the impact of technology on certain cultures but also with the impact of various rates of change and the sequences in which technological components develop and affect each other. Viewed in the Mankind perspective, spreading technology may lead to the creation of "technological misfits" within certain cultures.

Scientific and technological resources can be mobilized on behalf of the nation, but could the vast resources of technology be mobilized on behalf of Mankind? Believers think that the most significant task in the application of science to social problems is no longer the actual doing of applied research or even the training of people, but the making of the great decisions that determine the rate and direction of progress.

Bringing together technology and the humanities involves the question of values. There should be two basic value concerns: one having to do with fulfillment of the unknown potentialities of man, the other with the actual terms of life: the human condition. The notion of human potential has been drastically altered by science and technology. But what do they have to say about potentialities? Which are the biologically and which the culturally determined potentialities?

From the Mankind point of view, this raises another question: under what conditions, in what respects, and to what extent would leaders in science and technology—in cooperation with those in education, economics, psychology, philosophy, the arts, and other disciplines—give primary consideration to the interests of Mankind, as reflected in some of the aforementioned problems?

Believers are aware of the complexity of the question, but as the policy would probably be applied only in the evaluation of relevant major problems, neither the integrity nor the autonomy of the various branches of science and technology need be involved. What would be involved would be increased awareness of the role of science and technology in the Mankind-oriented world of the future. In the pursuit of these principles and objectives, the new leadership group of Believers would seek to promote the creation of a Mankind Science and Technology Council.

THE ARTS

The leadership group would want to learn what the arts —both applied and fine arts, including literature, the dance, and all the others—had contributed toward the attainment of a Mankind-oriented society. Or whether and to what extent artists had used their great imaginative powers to try to visualize the emerging forms of a new humanity. Or whether they even should be expected to promote a cause such as Mankind.

In viewing the future of human society on the one hand and the rich potential of the arts on the other, the leadership group may wonder whether such society could be attained without their help; indeed, whether the arts would not be meant to show the way. For who has greater natural awareness of Mankind; greater freedom from prejudice of race, color or creed; greater feeling for the equality of all beings, than the artist? Might he not be able to make his unique contribution, once he had gained abiding faith in Mankind?

The leadership group would encourage a series of conferences with artists and persons interested in the arts. Subjects under discussion might be:

> the thinking of artists concerning the perception of Mankind in creating and expressing new forms of art;

> the contribution artists could make in communicating the idea of Mankind to young persons throughout the world;

> the contribution artists might make toward the conceptualization of the future image of Mankind;

> the preparation, publication, and distribution of Mankind educational material in the arts;

> the global organization of artists representing a variety of cultures, which would stress the need to relate the creation of new art forms to the idea of Mankind.

Mankind leadership would urge the artist, in striving for the vision of unitary Mankind, to meet face to face the challenge of tomorrow. With faith in the destiny of Mankind, the artist would be able to see the new world in his panoramic vision and to interpret it in forms which only he can produce.

MORALITY

Believers would consider respect for the life and dignity of the individual person the basic moral principle of Mankind. Moral principles are already operating throughout the world, but they are segmental rather than Mankind principles. The leadership group faces the task of converting the moral segmental into the moral Mankind effort. How can Mankind morality give effective leadership toward the realization of the Mankind-oriented society?

With other relevant groups, Mankind leadership would study major moral and ideological issues from the Mankind point of view. Ancient beliefs, dogmatic claims, and traditional interpretations would be considered in their relation to Mankind. The possibility of developing new groups within separate religious organizations, to represent Mankind's moral and spiritual interests, should be given careful attention.

Such groups would cultivate a close and meaningful relationship with the hierarchy and the dogma of each religion. Their activities might take the form of sermons in religious settings, of open discussions in conference settings, of public debates in political settings—all closely related to the issue of Mankind morality.

Identified as Mankind divisions, these groups would have a purpose and significance of their own, embracing and at the same time overarching the hierarchies and dogmas of all religions. The new groups would carry on educational work designed to broaden conceptual limitations. They would try to work out formulas which, while giving the Mankind concept primary consideration, would hold inviolate the distinctive features of each religion.

Realizing that the Mankind Age is calling for a broader theological interpretation than any known in the past, liberal-minded segments of religious institutions might well cooperate. The Mankind educational mission would be designed to overcome the barrier of conceptual limitations of dogmatic and institutional tradition.

PHILOSOPHY

The Mankind leadership group would likely agree with the views of noted philosophers on the need for integrated knowledge. Teilhard de Chardin and Julian Huxley considered the integration of all knowledge (proposed by Aristotle, Bacon, and many others) as a prerequisite for the attainment of the orderly society. F.S.C. Northrop believes in unifying the ideas of East and West, others, in integrating psychology and biology, science and philosophy, art and economics. But whether it be Unified Thought (Whyte), Unified Science (Reiser), or the Doctrine of the Whole (Mumford), virtually all theories and philosophies of world order either are or eventually become all-inclusive schemes regardless of discipline.

Professor Richard P. McKeon of The University of Chicago has pointed out that practically every branch of philosophy is concerned with basic issues which can be rendered clearer by relating them to the idea of Mankind:

> *Legal and Political Philosophy* could be concerned with the development of new social and political institutions.
>
> *Moral Philosophy* might find the grounds of a fundamental ethical agreement in the conception of Mankind.
>
> *Logic* might clarify questions of language and communication when systems of logic are related to the operation of Mankind.
>
> *Metaphysics* can specify more clearly the relations of individuals to other minds, to things, events, or the universe, if it sees them in the perspective of Mankind.
>
> *Esthetics* may examine whether questions in artistic creation indicate aspects of esthetic value, depending on what is common to Mankind rather than individual innovation.[8]

The leadership group would seek to arrange, in cooperation with similarly oriented groups, a series of conferences attended by scholars, statesmen, educators, psychologists, jurists, anthropologists, students, and other interested persons. Participants might be expected to:

(1) prepare a summary report, including an outline of guideposts and principles for a Mankind philosophy;

(2) set up a special advisory group to plan the formation of a Mankind Philosophical Council;

(3) draw up plans for the organization and development of Mankind Philosophical Committees in different countries, which would implement, refine, and enlarge these and subsequent programs.

POLITICAL ACTION

Even if the various programs were planned, designed and organized in accordance with Mankind principles and along Mankind perspectives, a vital element would still be lacking: the broadly coordinated effort needed to create the Mankind-oriented society, which would assure conditions of order, peace, and justice throughout the world. Only under these conditions, Believers would insist, could the individual person be a citizen of Mankind, the only status giving him true political freedom.

These conditions are now controlled by national authorities, the affairs of which, in turn, are guided by interests advanced through political channels. The leadership group must therefore give earnest consideration to the need for organized political Mankind action. If Mankind projects are to have full and lasting impact upon a society intended to be Mankind-oriented, they must have broad political support throughout the world.

Believers place strong emphasis upon the absolute need for such organized support. When asked why, they will give three principal reasons:

(1) The improvements which Believers consider essential to a Mankind-oriented society, such as abolition of war, dignity of the individual person, and equal rights, are not likely to be enacted in any country without strong popular demand throughout the world. To be effective, this demand must be backed by Mankind education, Mankind motivation, and Mankind discipline. The only means of creating, developing, and maintaining such support on a substantial scale is through a tightly controlled party system.

(2) The forces of nationalism in one form or another are so powerful and so deeply rooted in the political, economic, social system of any country that they would squash any serious Mankind legislative proposal, as they have done in the past. Only the combined political strength of the people can deal successfully with these forces.

(3) Without organized political support, people throughout the world would have no clearly identified place where they could publicly debate major issues related to Mankind, or cast their votes for or against Mankind legislative proposals. There would be no better place for Mankind education and training than in such an organization.

In turn, Believers may be asked why existing organizations that have a Mankind orientation (either large ones such as United Nations, or smaller ones that are less well known) could not assume the functions of a political Mankind group. Why must it be a new organization? Believers would point out that, while United Nations is doing much good in many parts of the world, it is severely limited by the absence of a world authority and the prevailing rule of national sovereignties. It cannot serve as an effective representative of Mankind.

Hundreds of smaller groups striving for world peace and related Mankind objectives are composed of dedicated persons. Believers would explain their lack of success by ineffective leadership, use of inadequate methods and ineffective tools, spiritual over-emphasis, and lack of organization and discipline—all of which impede progress toward practical goals.

Mankind support could take other forms:

Individual persons could express their support for a Mankind-oriented society by voting for candidates of present political parties known to favor Mankind action. Could such candidates be found? Is enough known about the why and wherefore of Mankind needs and interests to justify any voting support at all? Does not the Mankind proposition presuppose a rather substantial amount of knowledge concerning the basic concept of Mankind, its origin, direction, and global implications? These and related questions seem to make the possibility of individual voting support rather doubtful.

National governments could create Mankind-oriented departments that would seek to broaden interest in the idea of Mankind and to help clarify the specific relationship of nation to Mankind. As a government agency, its natural and constitutional allegiance would be to its own government.

Thus, its interpretation of major issues and problems would likely reflect government attitudes, interests, and politics. Since the Mankind concept is based upon its universal nature as its primary and exclusive character, it is difficult to see how such department could function effectively as Mankind's national representative.

Political parties could write a Mankind plank into their campaign platforms. However, this plank would probably have a most difficult position in the actual campaign. The question of primary allegiance would be only one of the difficulties. The fact that Mankind must have primary allegiance would cause conflict with party as well as with national policies and constitutional principles. If the party were to be served first, the Mankind interest would have to take second place—which obviously would be self-contradictory.

Religious institutions could set up a form of Mankind representation within their own organizations. Indeed, it will be pointed out that their dogma contains a definite Mankind orientation. It finds ever repeated expression in theological interpretations of the faith as well as in prayers and other religious manifestations. Moreover, religious institutions are responsible for much charitable, welfare, and other activity, which is Mankind-oriented.

Political representation, however, would be a different matter. There is the traditional conflict between church and state. Organized political Mankind representation would complicate and might intensify the conflict. If such representation were established in a religious institution, it would have to be entirely free to work with both the religious hierarchy inside and Mankind leadership outside. In the Mankind sense, it could not be effective otherwise.

Industrial organizations might conceivably develop a form of political Mankind representation either through management associations or within their own, often elaborate structures. Since such representation would likely be supported by the industrial establishment, it is not easy to see how special interests, which the establishment already has or is eventually bound to have in world affairs, could be separated from the work of the special Mankind department. The latter would be expected to give its undivided attention to the interests of

Mankind. This might prove especially difficult if the latter should run counter to the interests of the organization sponsoring the work of the special agency.

These possibilities of organized political Mankind representation would seem unrealistic to Believers because a basic and most important condition could not be met: that is, complete freedom to act in allegiance to and in the interest of Mankind. No doubt, there are other forms in which political Mankind action could be expressed. They would probably suffer from the same basic lack of freedom. Barring future developments which might remove some of the aforementioned obstacles, the one feasible way of generating political Mankind action would seem to be for the Mankind leadership group to organize a

MANKIND POLITICAL PARTY

214
The leadership group could start this action by preparing a clear and precise statement setting forth proposed principles, objectives, and activities. The party's prime objective would be the representation of the Mankind interest in all major problems and public issues. To clarify the interest of Mankind, the group would seek to define what is good and what is bad for Mankind. An annotated summary of needs, interests, and aspirations would indicate what should be considered good for Mankind, and why. A corresponding summary of actions, motivations, and interpretations would indicate what should be considered bad, and why.

The group may find that what is good or bad for Mankind is not basically different from what is good or bad for society, nation, race, church, labor, and other groups. Violation of their respective codes is considered bad and therefore punishable, like stealing a car. Treason is considered bad for the nation; infringement of its ritual, bad for the church; disobedience of the worker, bad for the union. What is good, then, is what aids not only the survival but the advancement of the cause it serves. If the rule were extended to Mankind, what would be considered good would be that which promotes the welfare of Mankind, and what would be considered bad would be that which endangers the welfare, let alone the survival, of Mankind.

Because something is good for nation, church, labor, or other group, it does not necessarily mean that it is good for Mankind. In fact, it may be bad for Mankind precisely because it is thought good for nation (war), church (certain types of overseas missions), or labor (restricted immigration). The criterion for the leadership group would not be how good things might be for different segments but how good they could be for Mankind.

ALLEGIANCE

Among the important items on the agenda of the leadership group would be "Allegiance to Mankind." As previously stated, Believers think that unless Mankind is accepted as the primary concept, it cannot meaningfully represent the totality of man and his society. The foundation of the Mankind concept is its universality. To remain true to its character as well as to its promise, Mankind must have primary allegiance. In application of this principle, an early declaration by the leadership group might ask members of the Mankind Party to make certain commitments, among them:

215

(1) To pledge allegiance to Mankind and the World Community for which it stands: one society, indivisible, with freedom, order, justice and peace for all.

(2) To transcend the limitations of national, racial, tribal, ethnic, political, and other groups, so as to be able to rise to the concept of Mankind.

To see that none of the special interests of particular segments (nation, race, tribe, industry, labor, etc.) are carried to excess which would be harmful to Mankind.

(3) To represent the interests of Mankind. To ask of any major issue (atomic fall-out, pollution, drugs, tariffs, farm surplus, migration): "How would its passage or defeat in the legislature affect not only our country, other friendly, hostile or indifferent countries, but Mankind itself?"

(4) To cooperate with all and oppose none who are dedicated to the welfare of Mankind: nations and religions, cultures and institutions, artistic forms and scientific disciplines, United Nations, Friends, communists and capitalists. Individuality and diversity must be respected everywhere.

(5) To proclaim the sanctity of the human life. This principle makes no distinction between democracy and communism, between nationalism and fanaticism, between the crusades of Christians and the holy wars of Mohammedans. However holy the cause, it loses its holiness as soon as it causes one part of Mankind to destroy another. To Mankind, all human life is holy. One cannot take one life and not hurt Mankind. One cannot wipe out a hundred million lives and not threaten the survival of Mankind. The protection of human life is the highest moral law, as the taking of human life, for whatever reason, is the greatest crime.

(6) To reaffirm the basic human rights of the individual person— not as member of community, tribe, race, or nation, but primarily as member of the human race; not as belonging to a certain class, caste, or culture, but primarily as belonging to Mankind.

(7) To oppose imposition and intrusion upon the rights of others, whether they take the form of highly automated devices installed in primitive economies, religious missions in overseas territories, or sovereign rule upon subject people. To show concern for the affairs of other countries and other people; to be tolerant of their ways, ideas, beliefs, and aspirations.

PARTY TEAMS

In these and related ways, Believers and their leadership group would seek to work out the Mankind interest in principle. In practical application, the task would fall to special Mankind teams selected for the specific task they were called upon to perform. Teams might concentrate on three major areas:

(1) The organization of teams and the development of effective relations and attitudes:

   (a) between members of each team,

    (b) between members of different teams,
    (c) between teams and their anticipated collaborators outside the Party.

The purpose would be to develop not only a meaningful but a dynamic establishment for the effective operation of the program, as worked out by the Mankind leadership group.

(2) The selection, analysis, and preparation of Mankind issues:

    (a) to submit to the leadership group for its decision,
    (b) to prepare selected issues for full conference programs, with the cooperation of similarly-oriented leadership groups.

(3) The preparation of agendas and programs for the complete series of conferences and conventions—their proper conduct and management, their implementation and follow-up—organization of post-conference meetings, proceedings, and developments.

The character of the Party would be protected as well as strengthened by strict Party discipline, which should be worked out in careful detail. Party members on the various teams would be expected to adhere to it, not only as a matter of education and training but as an article of faith. Non-Party team members would be asked to respect it.

Those serving on Mankind teams would require special abilities. One might have to perform a special service for a specific task; another would be asked to explain the Mankind character. The ability for leadership, as stated previously, would be revealed by the depth of insight and compassion. Much wisdom and talent would be needed to find out whether and how democracy, communism, other isms could be related to a world constitution; whether and how local, state, national, and international laws could be related to world law, world ethics, a world authority; to find out what rights and responsibilities might govern a relationship between Mankind and its autonomous segments: nations, races, tribes, religions, cultures, institutions, political parties, scientific disciplines—not forgetting the individual person.

Any exclusive association with other organizations should be avoided so that the Mankind Party, through its various branches, could cooperate with all organizations while working out its own identity.

Routine activities of Party members would be geared to "Service for Mankind." They might include:

> Keeping major Mankind issues and problems constantly before the public.
>
> Raising Mankind questions in seminars of high school, adult education, college, and university groups.
>
> Challenging political candidates; circulating petitions; writing letters to the press.
>
> Carrying Mankind debates into intellectual circles and literary groups.
>
> Impressing the Mankind idea upon important persons in public life: statesmen, educators, authors, artists, scientists, and many others.
>
> Arranging meetings and conferences; enlisting members; organizing local chapters.

Some intellectual input should be provided. It would help the Party to justify its far-reaching aims against skepticism and hostility. Equally important would be financial support, coming mostly from the public and from segments of the world economy. The Party's prime objective of helping to attain conditions of order, justice, and peace on a global scale and in a Mankind framework would amply justify such support.

While leaders of local Mankind groups would be elected by Mankind Party representatives, members of the Supreme Advisory Mankind Council would be elected by representatives of the larger contingents. With the members of the Supreme Advisory Council would rest the power to decide how the basic requirements of faith, commitment, self-transcendence, and vision were to be adapted and readapted to the changing demands of time.

All these activities would be designed to deal with Mankind's most urgent problems. Their success would not only be the triumph of Mankind Believers or the Mankind Party or

Mankind leadership. It would be the triumph of Mankind itself, in realizing a society of justice, order, and peace. In a deeper sense, it would be the triumph of the people, in having created a world in which they could live in security and equality, in freedom and dignity.

Chapter One

1. J. D. Mackie, *The Earlier Tudors*, (Oxford: Clarendon Press, 1952), pp. 462-63.
2. *Ibid.*, pp. 470 ff.
3. Sidney A. Reeve, *Energetics*, 2 vol., *Social Energetics*, vol. II (Nyack, N.Y., 1939), pp. 186 ff.
4. Sidney Vere Pearson, *The Growth and Distribution of Population* (London: George Allen & Unwin Ltd., 1935), p. 172.
5. Henry Pratt Fairchild, *People* (New York: Henry Holt & Co., 1939), p. 60.
6. H. G. Wells, *The Outline of History* (New York: The Macmillan Co., 1921) pp. 204-6.
7. Leslie A. White, *The Science of Culture* (New York: Farrar, Straus & Co., 1949), pp. 378-79.
8. Arnold J. Toynbee, *A Study of History* (London: Oxford University Press, 1947), p. 211.
9. Pierre Teilhard de Chardin, *The Future of Man* (New York: Harper & Row, 1964), pp. 233-34.
10. M. M. Kovalevsky, *Contemporary Sociologists* quoted in Harry Elmer Barnes, *An Introduction to the History of Sociology* (Chicago: University of Chicago Press, 1948), p. 452.
11. Reeve, *op. cit.*, p. 165.
12. Harold Rugg, *Changing Governments and Changing Cultures* (Boston: Ginn & Co., 1932), p. 327.
13. White, *op. cit.*, pp. 169 ff.
14. William Fielding Ogburn, *Social Change with Respect to Culture and Original Nature* (New York: The Viking Press, 1933), pp. 90 ff.
15. Walther Rathenau, *Zur Kritik der Zeit* (Berlin: S. Fischer Verlag, 1912), p. 55.
16. Rugg, *op. cit.*, p. 307.
17. Reeve, *op. cit.*, p. 115.
18. Rugg, *op. cit.*, p. 309.

19. Edward Alsworth Ross, *Standing Room Only?* (New York: The Century Co., 1927), pp. 93 ff.
20. Charles Austin Beard, ed., *Whither Mankind?* (New York: Longmans, Green & Co., 1928), pp. 52 ff.
21. J. H. Robinson, J. H. Breasted, and E. P. Smith, *Earlier Ages* (Boston: Ginn & Co., 1937), p. 136.
22. Francis Galton, *Hereditary Genius* (London: MacMillan & Co., 1869), p. 346.
23. Pearson, *op. cit.*, pp. 396 ff.
24. *Views and Ideas on Aging*, Research Council for Economic Security, Publ. 103 (Chicago, 1955), p. 2.
25. Fairchild, *op. cit.*, p. 201.
26. J. J. Spengler, *Economic Growth in a Stationary Population* (Washington, D. C.: Population Reference Bureau, 1971), Selection 38.
27. Frank Lorimer & Frederick Osborn, *Dynamics of Population*, (New York: MacMillan Co., 1934), p. 196.
28. Raymond Pearl, *The Biology of Population Growth* (New York: Alfred A. Knopf, 1925), p. 158.
29. Herman P. Miller, *Population, Pollution and Affluence* (Washington, D. C.: Population Reference Bureau, 1971) Selection 36.
30. Quincy Wright, *Population and Mankind*, Special Paper (Santa Monica, Cal.: Council for the Study of Mankind), pp. 3-6.

Chapter Two

1. Cecil Roth, *A Bird's-Eye View of Jewish History* (Cincinnati: Union of American Hebrew Congregations, 1935), p. 11.
2. Stanley High, *The Church in Politics* (New York: Harper & Bros., 1930), pp. 56 ff.
3. Everett Dean Martin, *Farewell to Revolution* (New York: W. W. Norton & Co., 1935), pp. 66 ff.
4. *Ibid.*, p. 70.
5. J. W. Thompson, *The Middle Ages* (New York: Alfred A. Knopf, 1931), pp. 212 ff.
6. *Ibid.*, p. 273.
7. In ancient times, some political collectives had servant classes even in their early stages, notably in the form of

slaves obtained from conquered tribes. Until the nineteenth century, there was slavery in the United States. In some of the newly developing areas in Asia, Africa, and other areas, slavery exists today. However, these servant classes are not generally part of the original group; they form an added and extraneous segment. Sometimes, they are brought in because native people refuse to do what they consider degrading work. At any rate, the servant classes are outside the process which is here discussed: the change of the people from strong to weak.

8. Winwood Reade, *The Martyrdom of Man* (New York: Asa K. Butts & Co., 1874), pp. 319 ff.
9. Walter Millis, *The Constitution and the Common Defense* (New York: The Fund for the Republic Pamphlets, 1959), pp. 26-27.
10. Hamilton Fyfe, *The Illusion of National Character* (London: Watts & Co., 1940), p. 23.
11. C. Crane Brinton, *The Anatomy of Revolution* (New York: W. W. Norton & Co., 1938), p. 182.
12. Martin, *op. cit.*, pp. 192 ff.
13. Brinton, *op. cit.*, p. 182.
14. Sidney A. Reeve, *Natural Laws of Social Convulsion* (New York: E. P. Dutton & Co., Inc., 1933), p. 542.
15. Brinton, *op. cit.*, p. 182.
16. *Ibid.*, p. 184.
17. "Yet in the course of the last century the spread of education, the shortening and easing of working hours, the rise of unions and other more or less formal associations, the increase in experience with government forms and routines, seem to have increased the ability, if not the desire, of the poorer citizens to maneuver in the political sphere.

Nevertheless, these people are, in the main, indifferent to politics, although their indifference is not the classic, quiescent indifference of the tradition-directed. It is to a large degree the indifference of people who know enough about politics to reject it, enough about political information to refuse it, enough about their political responsibilities as citizens to evade them."

David Riesman et al., *The Lonely Crowd* (Garden City, N.Y.: Doubleday Anchor Books, 1950), pp. 196 ff.

18. "This discussion is intended to show not that mass democracy is more corrupt or less efficient than other forms of government (this I do not believe), but that mass democracy is a new phenomenon—a creation of the last half-century—which it is inappropriate and misleading to consider in terms of the philosophy of Locke or of the liberal democracy of the nineteenth century. It is new because the new democratic society consists no longer of a homogeneous closed society of equal and economically secure individuals mutally recognizing one another's rights, but of ill-coordinated, highly stratified masses of people of whom a large majority are primarily occupied with the daily struggle for existence."

Edward Hallett Carr, *The New Society* (Boston: Beacon Press, 1957), p. 75.

19. Brinton, *op. cit.*, p. 182.

20. Robert Hunter, *Revolution* (New York: Harper & Bros., 1940), pp. 221 ff.
21. *Ibid.*, p. 214.
22. J. H. Robinson, J. H. Breasted, and E. P. Smith, *Earlier Ages* (Boston: Ginn & Co., 1869), p. 135.
23. High, *op. cit.*, p. 57.
24. Reeve, *op. cit.*, p. 36.
25. Martin, *op. cit.*, pp. 174 ff.
26. High, *op. cit.*, p. 175.
27. Reeve, *op. cit.*, p. 28.
28. Oswald Spengler, *The Decline of the West*, 2 vol. (New York: Alfred A. Knopf, Inc., 1928), vol. II, p. 422.
29. *Ibid.*, p. 367.
30. Martin, *op. cit.*, pp. 209 ff.
31. Will Durant, *The Age of Faith* (New York: Simon & Schuster, 1950), pp. 637 ff.

Chapter Three

1. Pierre Teilhard de Chardin, *The Future of Man* (New York: Harper & Row, 1964), pp. 233-34.
2. *The Futurist*, February 1972, p. 16.

3. H. Guyford Stever, *The Futurist*, February 1972, p. 17.
4. Aspen Institute for Humanistic Studies, *The Futurist*, February 1972, p. 17.
5. Nathan Keyfitz, *National Populations and the Technological Watershed*, Special Paper (Santa Monica, Cal.: Council for the Study of Mankind, Inc., 1967).

Chapter Four

1. Charles Seymour and Donald Paige Frary, *How the World Votes* (Springfield, Mass.: C. A. Nichols Co., 1918), pp. 22 ff.
2. Jerome Davis, *Capitalism and its Culture* (New York: Farrar & Rinehart, 1935), p. 5.
3. Washington Irving, *Christopher Columbus* (New York: John B. Alden, 1887), pp. 77 ff.
4. Charles A. Beard, ed., *Whither Mankind?* (New York: Longmans, Green & Co., 1928), p. 51.
5. Seymour, *op. cit.*, p. 88.
6. Charles A. Beard, *The Idea of National Interest* (New York: MacMillan Co., 1934), pp. 113 ff.
7. Sidney A. Reeve, *Natural Laws of Social Convulsion* (New York: E. P. Dutton & Co., Inc., 1933), p. 455.
8. Reade, *op. cit.*, p. 33.
9. J. H. Robinson, J. H. Breasted, and E. P. Smith, *Earlier Ages* (Boston: Ginn & Co., 1869), p. 135.
10. C. Crane Brinton, *The Anatomy of Revolution* (New York: W. W. Norton & Co., Inc., 1938), p. 110.
11. Reeve, *op. cit.*, p. 503.
12. Durant, *op. cit.*, p. 649.
13. T. W. Arnold, *The Folklore of Capitalism* (New Haven: Yale University Press, 1937), p. 2.
14. Beard, *op. cit.*, p. 50.
15. James Burnham, *The Managerial Revolution* (New York: The John Day Co., Inc., 1941), p. 104.
16. Edward Alsworth Ross, *The Principles of Sociology* (New York: The Century Co., 1920), p. 506.
17. T. B. Macaulay, *Essays*, 2 vol. (New York: E. P. Dutton & Co., 1907), vol. 1, pp. 486 ff.
18. *Ibid.*, pp. 487 ff.
19. *Ibid.* p. 486.

Chapter Five

1. Otto Neurath, *Modern Man in the Making* (New York: Alfred A. Knopf, 1939), p. 88.
2. J. W. Thompson, *The Middle Ages* (New York: Alfred A. Knopf,1931), p. 239.

Chapter Six

1. Robert S. and Helen M. Lynd, *Middletown* (New York: Harcourt, Brace & Co., 1929), pp. 48 ff.
2. *The Futurist*, April 1972, p. 49.
3. Kimball Young, *Social Psychology* (New York: F. S. Crofts & Co., 1930), p. 361.
4. W. H. Cowley, *Three Distinctions in the Study of Leaders*, 1928 Journal of Abnormal & Social Psychology, XXIII, p. 151.
5. Lester F. Ward, *Applied Sociology* (Boston: Ginn & Co., 1906), p. 199.
6. Alfred Odin, *Genése des Grands Hommes* (Paris: Librairie Universitaire, 1895), p. 207.
7. Brinton, *op. cit.*, pp. 125 ff.
8. *Ibid.*, p. 124.
9. *Ibid.*, p. 126.
10. H. G. Creel, *Chinese Thought* (New York: The New American Library, 1960), p. 198.
11. Albert Edward Wiggam, *The Next Age of Man* (Indianapolis: The Bobbs-Merrill Co., 1927), pp. 153 ff.
12. Albert Edward Wiggam, *The Fruit of the Family Tree* (Indianapolis: The Bobbs-Merrill Co., 1924), p. 17.
13. *Ibid.*, p. 186.
14. Wiggam, *op. cit.*, pp. 221 ff.
15. Frederick Adams Woods, *The Influence of Monarchs* (New York: MacMillan Co., 1913), pp. 263 ff.
16. Horace Mann Bond, *The Tragic Waste of Talent*, Article, Chicago Sun Times, June 12, 1960, sec. II, p. 3.
17. H. Bergson, *Les Deux Sources de la Morale et de la Religion* (Paris: F. Alcan, 1933), pp. 333 and 373.
18. Arnold J. Toynbee, *A Study of History* (London: Oxford University Press, 1947), pp. 211-12.

Chapter Seven

1. Arnold J. Toynbee, *A Study of History* (London: Oxford University Press, 1947), pp. 300 ff.
2. Julian Huxley, *Evolution in Action* (New York: Harper & Bros., 1953), p. 36.
3. Ernst Cassirer, *An Essay on Man* (New Haven: Yale University Press, 1944), p. 24.
4. Theodosius Dobzhansky and Gordon Allen, "Does Natural Selection Continue to Operate in Modern Mankind?" *American Anthropologist*, LVIII, August 1956, p. 603.
5. "Love-energy not only increases the longevity of individuals, but also the life-span of societies and organizations. Social organizations built mainly by hate, conquest, and coercion, like the Empires of Alexander the Great, Caesar, Ghengis Khan, Tamerlane, Napoleon or Hitler, have had, as a rule, a very short life, a few years, decades, rarely a few centuries. . . . The longest existing organizations are the great ethico-religious bodies like Taoism, Confucianism, Hinduism, Buddhism, Jainism, Christianity and Mohammedanism. All of these organizations have already lived for more than one thousand years—some for over two thousand, and there are no clear signs of their dissolution in the foreseeable future. The secret of their longevity probably lies in their dedication to the altruistic education of mankind and, generally, to the cultivation of love in the human universe."
6. "Generally, the pacifying power of love appears to be the main agency which terminates the long and mortally dangerous catastrophes in the life of nations. A systematic study of all such catastrophes in the history of ancient Egypt, Babylonia, China, India, Persia, Israel, Greece, Rome, and of the Western Countries uniformly shows that all such catastrophes were finally overcome by a notably altruistic ennoblement of the people, culture, and social institutions of these nations . . . We must not forget that practically all the great religions emerged in catastrophic circumstances and, at their initial period, were first of all and most of all moral social movements,

227

inspired by sympathy, compassion, and the Gospel of Love. They set out to achieve the moral regeneration of a demoralized society." Pitirim Sorokin, *Main Currents in Modern Thought,* September, 1958, p. 6.

Chapter Eight

1. J. H. Robinson, J. H. Breasted, and E. P. Smith, *Earlier Ages* (Boston: Ginn & Co., 1869), p. 142.
2. "Later, with the cities, but younger than they, *burgherdom, bourgeoisie,* arises as the "Third Estate." The burgher, too, now looks with contempt upon the countryside, which lies about him dull, unaltered, and patient, and in contrast to which he feels himself more awake and freer and therefore further advanced on the road of the Culture. He despises also the primary estates, "squire and parson," as something lying intellectually below him and historically behind him. . . ."

"God hath shapen lives three,
Boor and knight and priest they be."

Oswald Spengler, *The Decline of the West,* 2 vol. (New York: Alfred A. Knopf, Inc. 1928), vol. II, p. 334.
3. Sidney A. Reeve, *Natural Laws of Social Convulsion* (New York: E. P. Dutton & Co., Inc., 1933), p. 463.
4. Ludwig Gumplowicz, *Outlines of Sociology* (Philadelphia: Amer. Academy of Political & Social Science, 1899), pp. 127 ff.
5. Frederick L. Schuman, *International Politics* (New York: McGraw-Hill Book Co., Inc., 1941), p. 71.
6. Gumplowicz, *op. cit.,* p. 178.
7. Harry Elmer Barnes, ed., *An Introduction to the History of Sociology* (Chicago: University of Chicago Press, 1948), p. 30.
8. Barnes, *op. cit.,* p. 353.
9. Mabel A. Elliott & Francis E. Merrill, *Social Disorganization* (New York: Harper & Bros., 1934), p. 1006.

10. William Graham Sumner, *Social Classes*—The Forgotten Man and Other Essays (New Haven: Yale University Press).
11. Lucien Lévy-Bruhl, "The Philosophy of Auguste Comte," quoted in Barnes, *op. cit.*, pp. 97-98.
12. H. G. Wells, *The Outline of History* (New York: The MacMillan Co., 1921), p. 782.

Chapter Nine

1. C. A. Beard and M. R. Beard, *A Basic History of the United States* (New York: New Home Library, 1944), p. 47.
2. *Ibid.*, pp. 17-18.
3. *Ibid.*, p. 27.
4. *Ibid.*, p. 195.
5. *Ibid.*, p. 20.
6. *Ibid.*, p. 23.

Chapter Ten

1. Pitirim A. Sorokin, *Social Mobility* (New York: Harper & Bros., 1927), p. 451.
2. Walther Rathenau, *Zur Kritik der Zeit* (Berlin: S. Fischer Verlag, 1912), p. 23.
3. Hendrik Willem van Loon, *Whither Mankind?* ed. C.A. Beard (New York: Longmans, Green & Co., 1928), p. 50.
4. Alleyne Ireland, *Democracy and the Human Equation* (New York: E. P. Dutton & Co., 1921), p. 113.
5. H. G. Creel, *Chinese Thought* (New York: The New American Library, 1960), p. 204.

Chapter Eleven

1. See also Gerhard Hirschfeld, *An Essay on Mankind* (New York: Philosophical Library, Inc., 1957), pp. 20 ff.
2. "Under the momentum of this universal trend (the obligatory drift toward organized procedures), the individual will indeed find himself churned into an ever smaller particle, into a minute and at length irreducible atom of the social system. As the significance of the individual is thus steadily diminished, his status and

identity must necessarily approach that of a statistical average, while at the same time the mass will become correspondingly enlarged and dominating in its new and terrifying totality."
Roderick Seidenberg, *Post-historic Man* (Chapel Hill: University of North Carolina Press, 1950), p. 13.

3. Melvin Kranzberg, Science, Technology, and the Unity of Mankind, ed. W. Warren Wagar, *History and the Idea of Mankind* (Albuquerque, N. M.: University of New Mexico Press, 1971) Council for the Study of Mankind, Inc.

Chapter Twelve

1. August Heckscher, "Humanistic Invention in the Post-Industrial Age," eds. W. W. Brickman and Stanley Lehrer, *Automation, Education, and Human Values* (New York: School & Society Books, 1966), pp. 180 ff.

2. W. Warren Wagar, *The City of Man* (Boston: Houghton, Mifflin Co., 1963), pp. 3-5.

3. Pierre Teilhard de Chardin, *The Future of Man* (New York: Harper & Row, 1964), pp. 72-74.

4. Karl W. Deutsch et al., *Political Community and the North Atlantic Area* (Princeton: Princeton University Press, 1957), pp. 83-84.

5. Robert Ulich, Address 16th National Conference on Higher Education, Chicago, March 7, 1961.

APPENDIX

1. Professor Louis Gottschalk, Dept. of History, University of Chicago, discussion paper, Council for the Study of Mankind: "Has There Been a Discernible Trend Through History Toward a World Culture? If so, what are its Discernible Components?"

2. William H. McNeill, *The Rise of the West* (Chicago: University of Chicago Press, 1963), pp. 752 ff.

3. Emile Benoit, "Interdependence on a Small Planet," Article in *Columbia Journal of World Business*, Spring 1966, p. 14.
4. *The Futurist*, August 1971.
5. Willard Gurdon Oxtoby, "The Post-Ecumenical Era," *Theology Today*, October 1966, p. 380.
6. Neil H. Jacoby, draft on world productivity for planned international conference "Impacts of Multi-National Corporations upon International Relations and the Idea of Mankind"—1969, Council for the Study of Mankind, Inc.
7. Robert Ulich, *Education and the Idea of Mankind* (New York: Harcourt, Brace and World, Inc., 1964), p. XVI.
8. Richard P. McKeon, Conference "Philosophy and the Idea of Mankind," Council for the Study of Mankind, Chicago, 1962, Special Report, pp. 1-3.

INDEX

234

236

238

239

For Product Safety Concerns and Information please contact our EU
representative GPSR@taylorandfrancis.com
Taylor & Francis Verlag GmbH, Kaufingerstraße 24, 80331 München, Germany